M000027959

It is not light that we need but fire.
It is not the gentle shower but thunder.
We need the storms,
the whirlwind,
and the earthquake.

FREDERICK DOUGLAS

God's Thunderclap!

PASTOR JOHN SYKES

Copyright © 2020 by John Sykes

Critical Mass Books
Davenport, Florida
www.criticalmasspublishing.com

Cover Design   Eowyn Riggins
Interior Layout   Rachel Greene

ISBN: 978-1-947153-22-6

The sound of gentle stillness after all the thunder and wind have passed ultimately will the Word of God.

JIM ELLIOT

Foreword

A FAMOUS 20TH century theologian once remarked that a good preacher has a Bible in one hand and a newspaper in the other. I suppose these days we might say the preacher should have a Bible in one hand and social media in the other. Of course, neither expression is meant to equate the value and authority of God's Holy Word with the mere musings of man.

The point is that someone called to declare God's truth to this generation must believe the Bible is not only relevant, but essential.

Back during the dark days of the First World War, British Prime Minister David Lloyd George said, "When the chariot of humanity gets stuck, nothing will bring it out of the mud better than 'the foolishness of preaching.'"

He was right.

In the year 2020 the world indeed got mired in the mud of pandemic and cultural crisis. This is why we need men of God, like Pastor John Sykes, who stand boldly for the Word of God. This book, *God's Thunderclap!*, was born out of a series of sermons delivered during the darkest days of the COVID-19 crisis.

Now available to readers everywhere, I am sure you'll be encouraged and inspired by what this unique servant of our Lord has to say.

David R. Stokes
Best-Selling Author and Retired Pastor
Fairfax, Virginia
December 2020

Contents

CHAPTER ONE

"To get your attention"

THE LIGHTNING FLASHES, then—comes the thunder. Actually, it's called a *thunderclap*. A couple of years ago, there was a social media service called *Thunderclap*. Basically a "*crowdspeaking* platform," it was a way to make social media messages go viral. So, anyone, whether with good or evil intent, could disrupt the social media world and make a "thunderous" impact. As it happened, too many evil folks were using it—the Russians and others. In fact, it's believed to have been a major tool used by Mr. Putin and the Russians to influence voting and elections here in the United States. Such was the power of

Thunderclap. But the *Thunderclap* media service was shut down in 2018.

As I prepared to write this book, God impressed upon me that what is going on right now in America and the world is, in a very real sense, God's Thunderclap. Thus, the title for this book.

God's Thunderclap.

A thunderclap is a roar, a bang, a blast, a boom, a pop, a clap, something loud, something sudden, something meant to get your attention. And what is going on in the world right now certainly meets that description. It's all a Big Bang from God. And it's no theory.

It's very real.

God has impressed upon me that this is something designed to get everyone's attention, because we live in a time when, sadly, it seems that churches desire political correctness more than spiritual holiness. The powerful and life-changing message of the Gospel has been too often watered down and sugar coated. It's like what one author a generation ago said when he talked about the great question asked by a great prophet named Elisha, "Where is the Lord God of Elijah?" The author, taking a cue from that question, asked: "Where are the Elijah's of God?" Where, indeed.

I spent a good deal of time researching *COVID-19*, aka the *Coronavirus*. I wanted to understand what it was and what has been happening. Let's take a little time in this first chapter to give you a thumb-nail sketch of what I've learned. I'm no expert, certainly not a scientist, but there is a lot of information out there and I will do my best to boil it all down for the purpose of this book.

First, it is said that the virus itself has been around since the early days of human history, and actually about a third of all the common colds that our children get are caused by a type of coronavirus. In fact, there are several types of this virus—at least eight—and four of them have been around for ages. But the other four have shown up just in the past few decades. So, we have a case where some of the manifestations of coronavirus have been around for thousands of years, but other forms have been with us only about 30 or 40 years. One of those new viruses we know as *SARS*. Another we know as *ebola*. And another we know as *MERS*.

Now, *Ebola* affects people with uncontrolled bleeding and severe intestinal issues. It had its most pronounced outbreak in Africa, but is under control these days. Both *SARS* and *MERS* affect the respiratory system, as does *COVID-19*. All of them can be deadly, especially if left untreated. All of them are also highly contagious—easily spread from person to person with the ever-present risk of reaching epidemic, or even pandemic levels.

The name *corona* is derived from a look at the virus through a microscope. It actually looks like a piece of art, and the shape surrounding it looks like a crown, which is where the idea of corona comes from. It is believed that the virus originated from bats. Interestingly, they hibernate in the winter. This is where it gets murky. The belief is that the virus came from bats to humans via those who were either handling snakes, or what they call *pangolins*—a type of anteater. Now, you may not know this, but these are among the most trafficked mammals in the world. In fact, in Asia, there is a popular (and illegal) market for what they consider a delicacy. It is also trafficked for medicinal purposes—and this is the connection with the current virus. It came from an illegal market in China. Possibly a snake had been infected by a bat.

And bats have a history of bringing misery to mankind.

There are two basic types of the coronavirus—the *L* and the *S*. One is not as dangerous as the other. So, when you hear of people who have the virus doing well, they likely have the type that isn't as potent.

As I said, the virus originated in China, an atheistic nation, and it is now affecting the entire world. In fact, we are in the midst of a global pandemic for the first time in more than 100 years. There are seismic ripple effects, as well. The stock market has been on a rollercoaster ride. Trillions of dollars have been lost. Businesses have closed. Unemployment has spiked. This thing has impacted more than 100 nations, but we can't gauge the full scale of things because many of those nations (e.g., Russia, China, North Korea) don't furnish truthful information.

Suffice it to say, millions have been infected and hundreds of thousands have died, or will die before we are out of this crisis.

Some people try to compare coronavirus to the seasonal flu. But we already know that it is at least ten times more fatal than the flu. Yes, of course, there have been times when influenza (flu) has been more deadly than it is these days. At the end of the First World War, something called the Spanish Flu infected nearly a third of the world's population at the time, more than 500 million cases, and resulted in the deaths of nearly 50 million people. But that plague was aggravated by the devastating effects of the war itself, leaving in its wake homelessness, death, other diseases, and even starvation. Fifty years ago, in the 1960s, a version of the flu reached epidemic proportions and killed more than a million people worldwide. And throughout history there have been plagues, things like small pox, the black death, cholera, and other highly contagious and extremely deadly diseases. So, in a sense, what we are dealing with today is not really anything new under the sun. But we have not faced this particular virus before and have not had the ability to develop immunity.

You see, viruses tend to be smart and creative. They love finding ways to overcome any defenses we build up. They change—mutate, if you will—and they are no respecters of persons. They definitely do not discriminate. So, we've seen millionaires and those in deep poverty, the famous and the nameless, and people of all races and creeds impacted by coronavirus.

CHAPTER TWO

"Charmin will not save you"

WE LIVE IN interesting times.

People are gripped with fear.

People are uncertain about the future.

People are fighting.

People are hoarding.

I saw one video of people actually fighting over toilet paper. One woman was trying to take a pack of the stuff out of another woman's shopping cart. Most stores have signs telling people to get only enough for two weeks, but some seem to want to get enough toilet paper to last the rest of the 21st

century. I was at a meeting with a friend of mine, recently, and he said, "If you don't think people are panicking, just try to find toilet paper at *Walmart*." But I've got a word for everyone: "*Charmin* will not save you."

Then there was the story about a man who, when we were just becoming aware of the enormity of the potential coronavirus crisis, went out and bought up all the hand sanitizer in his town and the surrounding ones, as well. He wound up with more than 17,000 bottles of the stuff, buying them for about $3.50 per bottle and selling them for $50.00 each. There have also been cases where people have paid $80.00 to $100.00 for small bottles. Masks became expensive, as well.

Racism is on the rise again. There are Asians who have been attacked because people are saying the Chinese caused this crisis. And, of course, there is the ongoing crisis of systemic racism that is being widely protested in cities across the country. There is no doubt that the pandemic has served to further aggravate and complicate race relations in America.

We are currently experiencing information overload. We are so bombarded with reports, some false and some true, that it is hard to figure out who, if anyone, is telling the whole truth. The crisis creates a culture ripe for manipulation. It is apparent that even modern man does not really know what to do when faced with something this big. And simply listening to this report or that one and the litany of talking heads out there will drive you crazy. That, in turn, will breed and build fear. It's like Jesus talked about in Luke chapter 21, when he described, *"Men's hearts failing them for fear."* That kind of fear quenches faith. That kind of fear paralyzes you and is inherently destructive.

Now, there is another kind of fear that it constructive. It does not paralyze. In fact, it mobilizes us. It prompts us to practical action. It is not irrational. It is beautifully rational. It is wise. It is prudent. And it takes precautions. We acted on this rational fear in our church, where we have many elderly people. As you know they are in a higher risk category when it comes to dealing with coronavirus. We did some things to protect and help them deal with the pandemic.

We certainly can't isolate ourselves completely and still be effective at doing what God has called us to do. We must be wise about it, but we also have to remember that God does indeed have a purpose for believers right now, even during this pandemic.

In fact, *because* of it.

I often tell people, "If you want to see what this world will be like when we're gone, just read the Book of Revelation." In that final chapter of God's Word, it talks about a third of the population on the planet being infected by some sort of pestilence, which literally means a disease that has become a contagious plague. It will be so bad that people will be begging to die, but unable to.

Now, when it comes to eschatology, which is a big word to describe the doctrine of "last things," I am what they call "pre-trib." This means that I believe there will be a glorious rapture of the saints before the awful time of tribulation described in Revelation takes place. So, I plan to be gone and with the Lord while all hell breaks loose on earth. But that is not what is happening. We are here. This pandemic is real. And there are some things we must do to help others during these troubled times.

The vast majority of people on this planet do not really know about the awesome God we serve, or what they think they know is all wrong. Some people "know" all about the God who wants to make everybody happy, comfortable, and prosperous, but they willfully reject any concept of God that includes things like wrath, judgment, and righteousness.

I'm convinced that this is the reason for God's current *Thunderclap.* It is a wake up call for the church, and the world, compelling us to look at life through a spiritual lens. And not just any spiritual lens—it is one designed by the Creator of all things. This is a wake-up call we ignore at our own peril. In this unique moment in time, everyone in the world is affected without exemption.

But God is in control—never forget that.

In the early days of the pandemic, I watched the President of the United States, a man who is usually about as cocky and arrogant as they come, giving a speech sitting at his desk in the Oval Office. He looked so very uncomfortable. It reminded me of the first time I preached a sermon. Yes, *that* uncomfortable. Why? Because the definition of uncomfortable is being out of one's *comfort zone*. And the President was definitely out of his, not to mention in way over his head.

He is not in control.

The Democrats aren't in control.

The Republicans aren't in control.

The rich and powerful aren't in control.

Hollywood actors aren't in control.

Super sports-star athletes aren't even in control.

People from all walks of life are isolating themselves and shutting down their lives for the time being. Money doesn't matter. Power doesn't matter. Influence doesn't matter.

Not if you have the virus.

CHAPTER THREE

"God always knows how to get our attention."

CORONA SUGGEST A crown—the idea of someone in authority. Of course, it makes me think of the One who is seated on the throne of God. The Bible tells us that all other crowns will be placed at his feet. So, even corona has to ultimately bow before Almighty God.

Either God is sovereign, or He is not. Either He is in control, or He isn't. We must decide. But then again, He is Lord whether we "decide" He is, or not. Objectively, we know this. But in a subjective sense, when we consciously "decide" or "affirm" His sovereignty over all things, it chases our fear away. Instead, we walk in His wisdom, knowledge, faith, and courage.

While I was pondering all of this recently, the Lord led me to the writings of the Prophet Joel. My oldest son, Thad, has Joel for his middle name. The name means "Jehovah is God." It carries with it the additional idea of "He who will command." Joel's father was Pethuel, a name that means, "Mouth of God" or "Persuasion of God." So, if you look closely at the genetics or DNA of Joel, he came from a father who spent his life trying to persuade people to do right in the sight of God. He was God's spokesman for right living. Then comes Joel, the son, and God told him, "I want you to give the people a message. I'm commanding you to do something, and then I want you to command them to act on what I'm commanding you to do."

Through Joel, God said, "Something is getting ready to happen, something the world in all its generations has never before seen. You can tell it to your children and everybody else, because their eyes have never witnessed this." Sound familiar? In fact, we are seeing something this generation has never before seen. We have never dealt with anything like it. And God, who had a hard time getting and keeping our attention so much of the time sent a Thunderclap!

The Thunderclap he chose to use was not loud like a bomb, or even large like an earthquake. No, He used something very small—even tiny. He said, "I am going to take little caterpillars, no bigger than a human finger, and they will come upon you by the billions and wipe out your crops and vineyards. They will crawl up your walls—and on your skin. You won't be able to fight or defeat them. No pesticide can stop them. And I will do this because...you have *forgotten* me."

There was another prophet around at the time. His name was Hosea, and he also hadn't been able to get the attention of the people. So, Joel wasn't alone. Hosea said, "According to their pasture, so were they filled; they were filled, and their heart was exalted; therefore, have they forgotten me."[1] They had been blessed with so much prosperity that they forgot the source of those blessings. They were living luxuriously and were filled with the pride of life. "I have a new house. I got that promotion at work. I finished that college degree. I built this church. I grew this ministry." That's how they felt. It was all about them.

They had totally forgotten something the Lord had said generations earlier to those who first occupied the Promised Land:

_____

[1] Hosea 13:6, KJV

"And it shall be, when the Lord thy God shall have brought thee into the land which he swore unto thy fathers, to Abraham, to Isaac, and to Jacob, to give thee great and goodly cities, which thou buildest not, And houses full of all good things, which thou fillest not, and wells digged, which thou diggest not, vineyards and olive trees, which thou plantest not; when thou shalt have eaten and be full; Then beware lest thou forget the Lord, which brought thee forth out of the land of Egypt, from the house of bondage." – Deuteronomy 6:10-12 (KJV)

God always knows how to get our attention. Whether it's through lightning or a "still, small voice," He knows how--and even more importantly—when. There are times when He says, "I'm going to allow destruction. I'm going to allow the locusts to swarm. I'm going to allow a bat to unleash a virus on mankind to shut down cities, nations, business, sports, economies, culture, and political power.

So, in our day, God is saying, "I'm going to allow a little virus, microscopically smaller than any grasshopper. Something insignificant, but it will get your attention. Oh, yes!" We may forget Him next month, but God certainly has our attention right now. Something infectious, contagious, and devastating has the globe in its grip. It's not merely sporadic, it's persistent and pervasive. And, as yet, there is no cure, and no way to prevent its spread outside of commonsense practices such as "social distancing."

But in a real sense, the people of God know what to do. Even though we don't have the answer, we know what to do. The world system is powerless and paralyzed. They haven't a real clue what to do. They bemoan the state of things. And I suppose there are some of the Lord's people who have gotten caught up in that. But those with spiritual discernment know how to go into the house of the Lord and cry out to the living God. We know how to proclaim a fast. We know that prayer changes things. It reaches past the heavens and to the very throne room of God. He hears the prayers of His children, and those fervent prayers of righteous men avail much. So, we are not hopeless or helpless.

We know how to pray for ourselves. We know how to pray for our friends and loved ones. We know how to pray for teachers and over our nation's classrooms. And we know how to pray for a country that has lost its way and doesn't have enough sense to even realize what is really happening. We, the people of God, know how to lock the refrigerator door, turn off Netflix and Hulu, and get down on our knees, humbling ourselves in the sight of God, knowing that He has the power to lift us up and change things!

Thunderclap
Rolling over waves of soil
and stones and leaves, wind
and rain reflecting off
the curling edges of heat and
clouds, the same air it tore like
cloth now drowns it oceanically
outward until the flash of
revelation conceived in the
embrace of heaven and earth
has become a low and gentle
plea against the ravages
of distance

PAUL CANTRELL

CHAPTER FOUR

"Just so much cosmic dust"

GOD IS TRYING to get the world's attention. You may be noticing that the normal arrogance of many politicians has been subdued, lately. As a matter of fact, we recently witnessed a miracle of sorts. Democrats and Republicans actually worked together. That's a miracle these days.

People who don't know God tend to respond to the current crisis in one of two ways. They either forget all about Him, or they *blame* Him. Have you ever noticed that the world likes to refer to natural disasters—things like hurricanes and earthquakes—as *acts of God*? Of course, that is far from true, because God created this world in a good state. God created this world perfect. It was man's sin that has affected the natural world.

It's all part of the reality of the law of sin and death.

God hasn't said, "I'm God, so I'm going to send a hurricane, or a pandemic." Not at all. In fact, when God created Adam and Eve, there were no hurricanes. There were no tornadoes. There was not even rain. There was no need for rain. God took care of everything. So, the things people call "acts of God"—things they can't otherwise explain or control––are actually the part of the fallout of sin in this fallen world.

God doesn't sit on the throne and say, "I'm going to send a tsunami!" But, does He allow it to happen? Yes, as collateral damage from the ravages of sin in our world. No sin; no tsunamis. No sin; no hurricanes. No sin; no tornadoes. No sin; no pandemic. It is sin that has brought calamity in the world. Plain and simple. So, I want to share some important reminders.

THIS WORLD IS PASSING AWAY

In First John 2:15-17, we find these words: *"Love not the world, neither the things that are in the world. If any man love the world, the love of the Father is not in him. For all that is in the world..."* Everything that's in the world, including you and me.

Anything we can see is going to be gone one day. Just so much cosmic dust. *"...the lust of the flesh, and the lust of the eyes, and the pride of life, is not of the Father, but is of the world. And the world passeth away, and the lust thereof: but he that doeth the will of God abideth forever."*

This is a reminder for people who are getting comfortable with their 401(k) accounts and their savings and just throwing a little something to God's work every now and then. Those who say, "I don't have anything else on the calendar, so I guess I'll go to church, and I hope the service isn't long today." It's a reminder that people have become so full of "the pride of life" that they don't have any time for God.

But it is more than a reminder—it's a loud roar. You see, everything around us—this material world—is going to pass away. Your house is going to pass away. Your backside is going to pass away. But, in great and glorious contrast, everyone who does God's will will endure and thrive. This is a time for inspection and inventory, a time to look at life through spiritual lenses, because everything is going to pass away. It's like the words of a song we used to sing when I first got saved: "Everything is going down but the Word of God." We must declare like Dr. King, the night before he died, saying "I just want to do God's Will!"

So, the first reminder is that everything is going to pass away. Matthew 24:6-8 says, *"And ye shall hear of wars and rumors of wars: see that ye be not troubled: for all these things must come to pass, but the end is not yet."* Man will continue to build bigger nuclear weapons. He will also make some more biological weapons. *"For nation shall rise against nation, and kingdom against kingdom: and there shall be famines, and pestilences [coronavirus?], and earthquakes, in divers places."*

A time of reckoning is coming. Our nation is at a crossroads. We are reaching the breaking point. Things we never thought could happen in the 21st century have been manifested in places like Ferguson, and in cities across the United States. But I believe God is saying, "Don't be troubled." It's just a reminder that judgment is coming.

It's His Thunderclap.

LIFE IS SHORT

After death comes judgment. There are two things to keep in mind: *certainty* and *uncertainty*. You're certainly going to die. The uncertainty comes from not knowing when, where, or how. But it's coming, of this you can be sure. Then after that, there's another certainty: you will be judged. People small and great. People from every imaginable background. It's an appointment that is already set. And you will be on time. It is one appointment you won't be able to text and say, "I'm running five minutes late." You won't be late.

It seems like just a few days ago I was in my 20s. I could run with the best, jump over hurdles, slay giants, and just about everything else. Now I have to pray myself over even small hurdles. Life is short and eternity is long. This is a reminder that I have to make sure everything is right down *here*, because I could get in the car today and be gone before I get home—and not have coronavirus.

Life is short.

MAN'S COMPLETE INSUFFICIENCY TO MEET HIS OWN NEEDS

Wall Street can't help us now. Don't put your faith in money. Politicians are trying to do their best, but what we have to realize is that God is our ultimate source. He is why I go to bed and sleep soundly instead of being up all night worrying about COVID-19. He is the reason that when I have a little cough, I just go get some water or a cough drop and go about my business, because it's allergy season. One of the hardest things in life is dealing with things over which we have no control. At such moments we reveal our complete human inadequacy. It's a humbling thing and the key is to take that humility and bring it to the Lord.

It's a sin for someone to price gouge at a time like this, charging $50 for a $2 bottle of hand sanitizer. I would hate to stand before God after doing that to my brothers and sisters. What we have to realize is that for us, as believers, this is a time to show the love of God and look out for each other. The world is hopeless and doesn't know what to do, but we as the people God know exactly what to do—show people the love of God.

People are looking for hope. They're looking for something to help them overcome their fears. They may lack hope, but *we* are not hopeless. The helpless lack help, but *we* are not helpless. This is an opportunity for us to see how we can be a blessing to those who do not know the Lord. We should be asking: How can I be a blessing to my brother? How can I be a blessing to my sister?

When I was putting material together for this book, I ran across a pastor who leads a church in Florida. They had a hurricane, and he talked about how one of his church members let him borrow a generator to help him keep his lights and his power on. He said he had a neighbor who didn't have a generator and who was about ready to lose all his food. So, he thought, *I'm going to be a good Christian.*

He told him, "You can plug up a cord into this generator someone was so kind to let *me* borrow, and then you can have your food and not lose your lights." He said, "I patted myself on the back. I'm being a good Christian. I did well." But the generator was running out of gasoline. He needed six gallons. So, he said, "I went to the gas station. There was a long line. I waited over an hour. I finally got there. He said, "I had a six-gallon container. When I got to 5.8 gallons, the pump stopped, and they made an announcement, 'We are completely out of gas." He thanked God that he got almost six gallons. A man behind him said, "Oh man! I've been waiting all this time, and I just needed a gallon. All I needed was a gallon, and I've been waiting all this time." He said, "I heard him, but I got my behind in the car with my 5.8 gallons, and I drove home." He said the Lord "whupped" him all the way home. The Lord said, "You passed the first test, but you sure enough failed the second one. If you had given him one gallon, you still would have had 4.8 gallons."

This is an opportunity for us to show love to others.

CHAPTER FIVE

"The Importance of Our Relationships."

THE IMPORTANCE OF family cannot be overstated. And it is so important to be right with each other. So often, we overlook this in our effort to succeed and acquire materials things. It helps us to realize that there is something more important than mere *things*: Relationships. *We are the light and the salt.*

We are salt and light and called to season and shine. We're to give hope when there's no hope. And we are to walk by faith. Sin isn't leaving here anytime soon, and there be ramifications and consequences. What we have to understand is that we have help through the power of the Holy Ghost. God has given us His spirit to help us deal with the world and its inherent sin.

Psalm 33:11 says, *"The counsel of the Lord standeth forever, the thoughts of his heart to all generations."* In other words, God doesn't do, or allow, anything to happen by accident. Whatever takes place, He has a purpose for it. God is never forced to tolerate anything. That's the God we serve. Our God is *intentional.* So, what's the intention? It's a wake-up call to look at life through your spiritual lens, because all natural disasters or pandemics are nothing but *thunderclaps* of God's grace and mercy, as He tries to get our attention so we will realize what's important in life.

China, where the coronavirus started, in Wuhan, is pretty much an atheist country. Christians are persecuted to a certain extent. My wife has experienced this and she tells me that they found that many times, the people of God would find out on Sunday where they were meeting. Sometimes it required long train rides to get to a place of worship.

It is interesting that in the place that was ground zero for this pandemic, the Christians in Wuhan, no doubt inspired by the Holy Spirit, have figured something out. Even though sharing the gospel is forbidden there, they have surmised, "If we have on masks, even with the cameras, they don't know who we are." So, if you go on the Internet, you will see Christians in Wuhan with their masks on passing out gospel tracts. They're sharing the gospel with their masks on. They say, "It's safe for us. They can't arrest us because they don't know who we are."

The fact is that Jesus saves! He is the answer! The answer is not a vaccine (though it's great that work is being done on that front), it is Jesus. If our brothers and sisters in Wuhan can risk their lives to tell their fellow citizens about the Savior, what are we doing walking around as if we are scared of our own shadows?

This is our opportunity to share the good news and ask folks, "Do you want to know why I have peace? Do you want to know why I'm still smiling? Do you want to know why I sleep at night? Do you want to know why I'm not scared? It's because I know Jesus, and He is large and in charge."

So, I say to the Body of Christ, this is our moment to stand up and also our moment to pray. We should pray for every nation. We should pray for the leaders of every nation. We should pray for every family that has been affected. People still don't get it. They thought it was so great on the news that in Italy, although they're locked down, they had a countrywide singing of the national anthem. I told my wife, "They should have a countrywide prayer meeting or at least be singing *Amazing Grace* or *Rock of Ages*."

Pray for the political leaders. Pray for the world. Pray for the scientists, that God will give them the wisdom and the knowledge to come up with a medical solution. The MERS, which is one that affected mainly folks in the Middle East, went away by itself. This was in 2014. We never came up with a cure. It just went away.

So, if God wants to say, "Go away"; if God wants to say, "Cease"; if God wants to say, "Die…" it could happen. Normally, when a virus reaches humans, it doesn't live, but this virus is able to jump. But God can say, "Jump back. Go back to the bats from which you came."

Pray for a cure, or pray at least that the spread of the disease slows down. Pray for those who are now ill, that God will bring healing to them. Pray that there will be no medical shortages, whether ventilators or tests or whatever is needed. Pray that this plague will go away in Jesus' name, and pray that after it's over, people will be willing to take another look at God.

Let me give you a final reminder in this chapter. There is a place. I've heard about it. I've read about it. I've heard songs about it. In this place, there will never be a pandemic. There will never be pestilence or disease. There is a place where there will be no sickness and no coronavirus or any other virus. There is a place where I won't have to worry about anything. The Bible says we won't even study war. There is a place where everybody is healed and filled, and all will have life eternal. There *is* such a place. But if I want to get to that place, I have to trust Almighty God, because He is the only one who can help me.

Life brings its thunderclaps. And God comes to us through these thunderclaps. He also comes through whispers. On Mount Sinai with Moses, it was a thunderclap. With Elijah on Mount Horeb, it was a whisper. God can come rattling like thunder, or He can come in a whisper; intangible, altering, shaking, moving, bold, and powerful. That's God.

Thunderclap!

To politicians, religious folks, China, Russia, and the United States, God is saying, "Can you hear me now? Do I have your attention?"

CHAPTER SIX

"Intentional Living"

FIFTY YEARS AGO, things were pretty bad in America. The Vietnam War was engaging, and it brought conflict home to the streets of our nation. There were protests—at time violent ones. The National Guard opened fire on students at Kent State University in Ohio, killing four. The drug culture was entrenched in our society. It was also a vital time for the civil rights movement. Back then, the world appeared to be conflicted and confused. It sounds eerily similar to today's world. Marvin Gaye's hit song, "What's Going On?" resonated then. And it is good refrain for our world right now.

In fact, it's prophetic.

When we look around, we see schools closing. We see colleges closing. We see businesses closing. We see restaurants closing. People who have spent tens of thousands of dollars for weddings have had to cancel their plans. Economies are grinding to a halt around the world.

We have seen shortages that we never imagined we could face. Things like N95 masks. And we will never forget the great toilet paper wars of 2020, where people hoarded four to five months of the stuff, so others couldn't find it, thinking somehow that would keep them safe and able to handle the virus.

Crazy.

We are facing financial meltdown, electoral disruption, medical breakdown and emotional distress. It seems as if the whole world is falling apart at its seams. I have even heard that large banks, such as J.P. Morgan, are paying their tellers a $1000 bonus to simply keep coming to work to handle the money, because no one wants to touch it for fear of infection. Talk about dirty money.

The *COVID-19* crisis has reordered everything. It has reordered our society in dramatic and dynamic ways. Look at the way travel has changed. Airports are virtually shut down. Travel has, for the most part, ground to a halt. Doctors and nurses are on the front lines. Military personnel are on the front lines. When this crisis has passed, I hope we remember to tell these heroes, "Thank you for your service!"

During this crisis, as we look around at our ever-changing society, we try to figure out what is going on. We have so many questions. What are we afraid of? What are we worried about? Are we humbled by the fact that there are things we cannot control? Are we humbled by the fact that something microscopic, that can't even be seen by the natural eye, that came from a filthy animal, is threatening to ruin the whole world as we know it?

March Madness is gone. Sports are trying to comeback—but without fans in the stands. It seems that everything familiar is fading away. We have gone through a major shock, one that has destabilized our economy, and that of the rest of world. What is going on?

2020 was supposed to be a great year. I was recently looking at some of the things that godly men had predicted for this year. According to them, 2020 was to be a year of *perfection*. A year of breaking through, a year of joy, and a year of supernatural shift. With all of those encouraging, positive words, we should ask, "What happened that so many were not able to see this?"

Well, come to think of it, we may be seeing that "supernatural shift."

CHAPTER SEVEN

"Seize the day"

IN SHAKESPEARE'S PLAY, *The Tempest*, a man said, "What's past is prologue." Indeed, it is. And we can learn a lot from history. Social distancing actually started more than a hundred years ago in St. Louis during the Spanish flu. The Spanish flu originated in Kansas and quickly infected those at Fort Riley. From there, during the waning days of World War I, it spread to much of the world. Interestingly, it is called the Spanish Flu because the first newspaper reports about it in America were about the illness of the King of Spain in May 1918, giving the impression that was where it all started. And a war-driven media black-out, here in the United States, made that explanation "convenient." There was a wave, and just when they thought it was over and they were through the worst, there was another wave. As the second wave was emerging, the people of St. Louis decided to do something that no other city had done.

They shut their city down.

It is said that, at the time, John Glennon, the Roman Catholic Archbishop of St. Louis, was furious with the health commissioner for this action. Everything was shut down except morgues, coffin manufacturers, grocery stores, drug stores, and saloons. That's right, you could go out for a drink, but not to church. However, because of this process, St. Louis was able to shut down the Spanish flu in a matter of three months.

At that time, St. Louis was the sixth largest city in America. And through their bold action, they stopped the spread of the Spanish flu in the American Midwest. By way of contrast, other cities that did not take such drastic measures suffered immensely. But St. Louis was the place where social distancing was started and it proved to be successful. Still, even with these measures, they still lost 2,000 people to the sickness. People died in hospital waiting rooms. People died in their buggies and in their homes. They did not have the technology we have today. But through their pioneering efforts, they were able to bring the spread of the deadly illness under control.

Did you know that a male is two to three times more likely to die of coronavirus than a female? If you are a male and a smoker, and you are hospitalized for *COVID-19*, there is about an 80% chance that you will survive. There is a direct correlation between being a male smoker and death from the virus. It is believed that women, because of estrogen, are better able to fight off the virus.

As I was studying these types of illnesses, I learned that our last resistance occurs when our T cells and B cells are released to fight off whatever is coming at us. During the Spanish flu, the people who died were mainly younger people, between the ages of 20 and 40, because they were so strong. It is believed that the Spanish flu actually came from pigs, therefore, many pig farmers died in Kansas.

Because the men were so strong, their bodies *overreacted*. When a body overreacts, when you're hit with the virus and the T and B cells are released, sometimes it brings on great inflammation and death. Women have a much better chance of surviving, because estrogen prevents the T and B cells from being released, in many cases.

So today, if you are a male smoker and you contract this virus, you had better start saying your prayers. Ladies, you are not necessarily out of the danger zone. Women are dying. But in China, Korea, and all over the world, men who are smokers are dying at a much higher rate than women.

As we are dealing with this virus people are wondering, "Will I have a job? Will I have food? Will I be able to pay my bills? What will I do?" And to top it all off, kids are now at home all the time, and it's driving many people crazy. I have been telling families that they had better take a lot of walks and spend time outside. It is hard to go from a life where everyone goes their own way and does their own thing, to a life where whole families are cramped in the house, with nowhere to go, not even school or church.

We have been hit with, what I call, *bioterrorism*—a terrorist act called *coronavirus*. I came up with an acronym for coronavirus, and what we are facing because of it: Cancelling Our Routine, Overtaking National Agendas, Victorious In Rendering Us Sick.

ONE DAY

Matthew 6:34 says, *"Take therefore no thought for the morrow: for the morrow shall take thought of the things of itself. Sufficient unto the day is the evil thereof."*

The first reason we cannot take much thought about tomorrow is that we don't control tomorrow. We have no guarantee that we will be here tomorrow. You have probably heard the saying, *Carpe Diem*. It means, "seize the day." In other words, because we don't have control over what will happen tomorrow, we have to do the best with what we do have, which is today.

I have a little saying on my desk. It is a cartoon. It says that you have to do your best today, and it says, "That's why it is called, the *present.*" Each day is a gift. Each day you have a present—*today.* You must do the best you can today, because there will come a time in all of our lives when tomorrow will not come. So be intentional about today. Why? Because the Bible says, "Sufficient unto the day is the evil thereof." In other words, during this time of coronavirus, we all have enough trouble today. We do not need to worry ahead about Monday's trouble, Tuesday's trouble, Wednesday's trouble, or any day going forward.

Everything has changed.

There were things that we did a few months ago that we never dreamed we would be hindered from doing today. But we have. There are many things that we are used to doing that we are not able to do now. In the past, old folks used to use the phrase, "If it be the Lord's will." They knew how fleeting the things of life could be. Maybe we should bring back that saying. "If the Lord is willing."

Second, The Bible says, "Take no thought for tomorrow." You cannot control this crisis. I cannot control the crisis. I cannot control what tomorrow will bring. One of the things that we have learned is that one day can change the world forever. The events of 9/11 changed the world forever. December 7, 1941 changed the world forever. The atomic bomb dropped in August 1945 changed the world forever. *Facebook* changed the world forever. The Lord wants us to simply dwell on today. Why? Because third, today will *never* come back. We cannot get back yesterday.

So, what do we do while where are camped up and shut in? The days are long. We have to watch old sports broadcasts that we have already seen. I turned the television on recently and I was like, "I don't want to look at the 1968 World Series. Come on here. Help a brother out!"

So, what *can* we do today? We can pray. There are no excuses. We have more time to pray. We have more time to encourage. We have more time to devote to God and to reading His Word. I have thought about what I would do if this was my last day, and I knew that it would be the last day I'd be alive. What would I do differently? I would start calling folks that I cared about. I would start texting my friends. I would reach out, and I would tell them how much I love them, and how important they had been in my life.

To those who had offended me, I would say, "I forgive you." To those I had offended I would say, "Please forgive me." I would try to give those around me an encouraging word. I would let them know that even though I am leaving them, there is hope. I would tell everyone, "Keep on trusting in Jesus.

Don't give up on God." If today was my last day, I would reach out to the unsaved. I would reach out to my loved ones. If today was my last day, I would encourage and help others.

CHAPTER EIGHT
"One day at a time"

WHILE WE ARE shut up in our homes, we can act like it's our last day and start doing what we would do if it really were our last day. The words "I love you" would come out of our mouths more often. The words "I forgive you" would come out of our mouths more often. The words "My bad" and "I'm sorry" would come out of our mouths more often. "I was stupid. I was arrogant. I was pompous. I was full of pride. Forgive me." These words would flow from our hearts and through our lips.

We should do these things today because God will meet today's needs. God knew about COVID-19 in 2019. God knew about coronavirus COVID-19a thousand years ago. God knew about coronavirus a million years ago, a billion years ago, a trillion years ago. We serve a God who has never been caught off guard.

He did not wake up one day and say, "Oh, I've got to change my plans and put something in place, because I forgot that in 2020 COVID-19 is going to take over the world." He was not surprised. Therefore, we must do something. We can't just shut ourselves in in fear and do nothing. God knew ahead of time what to do, and I guarantee that God will take care of you. But what should we do? We should look for opportunities today to do something that will affect others, help others, and lift others up.

There are lyrics to a song that say:

One day at a time, Sweet Jesus
That's all I'm asking of you
Just give me the strength to do everyday
What I have to do.
Yesterday's gone, sweet Jesus
And tomorrow may never be mine
Lord help me today, show me the way
One day at a time.

During COVID-19, we have to take life one day at a time. Opportunities are here. So, look for opportunities to help someone, encourage someone, and do good to others, because all we have is today.

ONE STEP AT A TIME

Psalm 37:23 says, "The steps of a good man are ordered by the Lord: and he delighteth in his way." The *New Living Translation* of this verse says, "He delights in every detail of their lives." And in Psalm 119:133, it says, "Order my steps in thy word; and let not any iniquity have dominion over me."

The word, *step*, is defined as a "measure of action; a course of action; an act or move or an action." A step is not as big as a jump. One step means a small action, or a small movement. How do you walk? One step at a time. A step implies small progress. In the Bible it refers to conduct. The Lord is saying that we have to be consistent. We must be deliberate. We are to be intentional about our next move.

The governments are so confused. They are trying to look into the future to figure out what their next move is. "What's the next move?" "Do we offer a bailout?" "Can we get companies that normally manufacture cars to make ventilators instead?" During the Spanish Flu in St. Louis, the *Red Cross* stopped making bandages and started making face masks and four-page pamphlets to be given out in eight different languages to help people.

So, today we ask what is our next step? What do we do? We are shut up in our houses. Our businesses are shut down. I believe The Lord is saying that during this time we have to calm down and realize that we cannot take one massive step that is going to overcome this crisis. We are going to have to take baby steps right now. One small step at a time. And you may be asking, "How do I stay sane?"

In fact, we may have to take it one *hour* at a time, in order to keep from being so full of worry.

The Bible says, "The steps of a good man are ordered by the Lord…" David said, "Thy Word is a lamp…." The Holy Spirit will guide us. He will lead us. God's Word will direct us. Faith is taking one step at a time and trusting that if we are walking in the will of God, even when we look down the road, and it seems like there is an open place with no solid foundation, God will provide the bridge for us to safely cross. When there is no way, God will make a way, and when we take the step.

This is faith.

In life we will take difficult steps. In life we will take easy steps. In life we will make missteps. But no matter what we face, God wants us to be willing to let Him direct our steps. We have to be intentional about this. We can't change everything in one day. Coronavirus is not going to go away in one day. But one day at a time, and one step at a time, we can take steps to keep our sanity. To keep our peace. To keep our joy. To not allow our faith to waver. It is simply done one step at a time.

The *Brooklyn Tabernacle Choir* said it this way:

Order my steps in Your Word, dear Lord
Lead me, guide me every day
Send Your anointing, Father, I pray
Order my steps in Your Word.
I love the next verse:

The world is ever changing
But You are still the same
Please order my steps, Lord
And I'll praise your name.

"The world is ever changing." We are seeing it now. We are seeing famine. We are seeing pestilence. There are wars and rumors of wars. There are illnesses such as COVID-19, SARS, MERS, Ebola. Yet, every step I take is being ordered by God. It is God who is directing me, not my fears. It is God leading me, not the world around me. It is God speaking to me, not the voices of those who fear. It is God helping me. That is why

I am not losing my mind. That is why I have peace that surpasses all understanding and joy unspeakable. Because my steps are not being ordered by a virus. My steps are not being ordered by what the President and other politicians do or won't do.

My steps are ordered by God.

CHAPTER NINE

"One true Gospel"

GOD IS ORDERING our steps. It is done one day at a time. One step at a time. When we allow Him to do this, we have peace. All of a sudden, we have joy. We no longer have to sit in front of the television 24 hours a day, listening to the media saying the same things over and over, as talking heads move from channel to channel.

The same faces that are on *MSNBC* at 9:00 are on *CNN* at 10:00. Then on *Fox* at 11:00. We need to turn that stuff off. At some point we have to say, "Lord, order our steps."

Ephesians 4:4-5 reminds us, "There is one body, and one Spirit, even as ye are called in one hope of your calling; one Lord, one faith, one baptism…"

ONE HOPE

During the time of COVID-19, we don't have two hopes. We have one hope. Hope is being certain of a good outcome. Hope is being certain about what you expect. Hope is believing that something pleasurable will happen in the future. Hope is believing that if I just wait for my change to come, God will show up.

1 Peter 1:3-6 says, "Blessed be the God and Father of our Lord Jesus Christ, which according to his abundant mercy hath begotten us again unto a lively hope by the resurrection of Jesus Christ from the dead…" We have hope. Hope is for the present. It is often said that you and I can live without anything but hope.

You do not have to have a mansion. You do not have to have a luxury car. You do not have to have a six-figure income. But you must have hope. People give up when they lose hope. The Bible says that you and I have a *lively* hope—that means a *living* hope. A living hope means that death is not the end. A living hope is sure. A living hope is certain. A living hope is a hope that never dies. A living hope is alive.

And a living hope is real.

A living hope is a promise of a better tomorrow, regardless of what is happening today. God says we have a living hope. This hope is not based on medication. It is not based on a ventilator. It is based on a *resurrection*. The resurrection of our Lord Jesus Christ. A living hope is a present hope. You can place your faith in Jesus, and in God's protection, and His Word. If the worst should come, it just means that I cease breathing here and that my next breath will be in eternity.

1 Peter 1:5 goes on to say, "...who are kept by the power of God through faith unto salvation ready to be revealed in the last time. Wherein ye greatly rejoice, though now for a season, if need be, ye are in heaviness through manifold temptations: that the trial of your faith, being much more precious than of gold that perisheth, though it be tried with fire, might be found unto praise and honour and glory at the appearing of Jesus Christ."

A living hope is a future inheritance that won't fade. It won't perish. It won't spoil. I am going to give you an example. A living hope is not you holding God's hand as much as it is God holding *your* hand. The Holy Ghost gave me this revelation when my sons were little. Sometimes when we crossed the street, I would hold their hands and tell them, "Now don't run out in the street. Hold my hand, and don't run out there."

Depending on their age, and how distracted they were, they might obey and they might not. But I, Daddy, was not worried. Do you know why? Because I knew that if they let go, I was still holding on to them. A living hope is not so much you holding on to God's hand as much as God saying, "You're mine." We have an inheritance that is incorruptible and undefiled, no matter what we do. And God is saying to us, "I am holding on to your hand."

Not only do we have a living hope, but we also have a calling. What is your calling? It's the plan for your life. God has a plan for every one of us. Your call is your conduct. Your call is the way you walk. There is a certain way we expect police officers to conduct themselves. We don't expect policemen to rob folks and beat people up. We expect them to serve and protect. We expect a doctor to heal and to take care, not to kill. A farmer is to produce crops.

A saint of God is to exhibit the fruit of the Spirit in their daily conduct. That is our calling from God. We are to be conformed into the image of God. We are to live out this calling daily. In these times, people don't need to hear us talk about how bad it is. They don't need to hear our fears. They need to see Him, and our hope in Him.

Each day your call is to act like a saint. Your call is to talk like a saint. To walk like a saint. To love like a saint. When you do that, those who don't know God will get to know Him because of the walk, talk, and love that you are exhibiting. So, we have one hope, and one calling.

ONE GOSPEL

Galatians 1:6-9 says, *"I marvel that ye are so soon removed from him that called you into the grace of Christ unto another gospel: which is not another; but there be some that trouble you, and would pervert the gospel of Christ. But though we, or an angel from heaven, preach any other gospel unto you than that which we have preached unto you, let him be accursed. As we said before, so say I now again, if any man preach any other gospel unto you than that ye have received, let him be accursed."*

In this day and age, there are many gospels vying for our attention. There is the gospel of success. There is the gospel of wealth, where God wants everyone to be wealthy. The people who proclaim this gospel even claim that Jesus was wealthy because the clothes he had on were not cheap. He always had money when He needed it. I've heard people try to break the life of Jesus down in a way to show that Jesus was not poor, but wealthy.

There is the "lite" gospel. This gospel says that we need to make the message of Jesus very friendly and not offensive to anyone. Those who proclaim this believe it is perfectly acceptable to water down the truth.

The noncommittal gospel says that coming to church is not important. Just accept Jesus as your Savior and then do whatever you want.

The inclusive gospel says that even if you don't accept Jesus, you are still saved. Everyone is saved. As long as you believe in a god you are saved. A sincere belief is enough. Yet how many of us have been guilty of sincerely believing something that was wrong. I am sad to say that there will be a lot of people spending eternity in hell because they were sincerely wrong about what they did and about what they believed.

God says that there is only *one true gospel.*

When people are trained to spot counterfeit bills, they do not study thousands of fake bills. They study genuine bills—the real thing. So, when they see a counterfeit, they know it is fake because they are so familiar with what is real.

The true Gospel, the good news, is the answer to all of our troubles. When people are terrified. When folks are anxious and don't know what to do. When you can't sleep at night. When we face hopelessness and are fearful of the unknown and the uncertainty (which is the foundation for most of our fears). When stomachs are turning and heads are aching, and we can't seem to keep our balance. Through all of this, we can know that God has given us the remedy. To get our balance back. To get our focus back. To get some peace. It is the gospel. The good news.

The true Gospel is not unfamiliar with turmoil. Have you ever read the book of Acts? Or Romans? The Gospel is not unfamiliar with what we are facing now, with the things that are happening in our world. We have good news. We do not need to sit around, covering our heads, talking about how scared we are. In fact, the more terrible things become, and the worse it gets, the greater the opportunity that we who know the real gospel have to say, "You can't make me doubt Him, because I know too much about Him."

In a time when the world is confused and lacking direction, and doesn't know what to do, we can quarantine ourselves. But we cannot—and should not—quarantine the gospel. We are not ashamed of the Gospel of Jesus Christ. So, while we may have social distance, this does not mean that we must have *disengagement*. We can tell everyone who is afraid of being on a ventilator about God's ventilation system. What does a ventilator do? It helps you breathe. It gives you breath. But God provides the very breath in our lungs! God has an eternal ventilator called the *ruwach* or *the breath of God*.

It is the Holy Spirit.

Ventilators do not heal you. They simply allow you to keep breathing while doctors try to find a way to heal you. But you don't have to wait to find an antibiotic. When you have the

Spirit of God on the inside, man may say that you stopped breathing, but God says that you have eternal life. I have learned that eternal life cannot be eternal if it stops for a second. This means that I will never, ever stop breathing. This is good news! It is worth telling others.

For the saints, we must experience contact without contamination and separation without isolation. We have to let people know that we have experienced an eternal resuscitation. If you have put your trust in Christ, and you are saved, you have received an eternal ventilator, so there is no need for us to hide and be scared of anything. God has got me!

Times of great calamity and confusion have been productive for the greatest minds. The purest ore is produced from the hottest furnace, the brightest thunder-bolt is elicited from the darkest storm.

CHARLES CALEB COTTON

CHAPTER TEN

"Risktakers"

BEFORE JESUS LEFT this earth, He gave us one command. Go and tell. Go and share the good news. Tell all people that there is something we have that can help. It's the Gospel. I know life can be scary. But when we think about it in light of what God said, and think about the good news of the gospel, and what we have in our possession, we don't have to be scared. The devil can't take it away from us. We have a living hope and an assurance.

The Lord said, "In my Father's house are many mansions, and if it was not so, I would have told you. I'm going there to prepare a place for you." Have you ever truly thought about that? I have, and I realized that I have good news that *Fox* doesn't have. That *CNN* doesn't have. That *MSNBC* doesn't have. I have good news that the enemy doesn't have. You can be healed. You can be forgiven. You can be saved. You can inherit eternal life.

As saints, this is our great opportunity. This is fertile ground. The more confused people are, the more powerful the gospel can be for them. The more hopeless they are, the more powerful the gospel. The more suffering that they face, the more powerful the gospel. This is the time when the saints need to crank it up and shout the good news.

It is said that sometime between AD 250 and 270 there was a plague that went through Rome. The Roman Empire dealt with a plague that is much worse than what we are dealing with today. The Romans believed that the plague was brought on by the Christians, so they persecuted the Christians.

A group called *The Parabalani* rose up and performed selfless deeds. They drew their name from Paul's letter to the Philippians, and how a man named Epaphroditus had risked his life to help him. The word risk comes from a Greek word: *parabouleúomai*. So, *The Parabalani* was a band of risk takers. They were "special ops" Christians who would go into dangerous situations maybe facing illness, peril, or risk, in order to advance the cause of Jesus Christ. In the year 252 AD in the city of Carthage, North Africa, as the plague was killing people by the thousands, people were afraid to go near the dead bodies. So, the diseased remains were not being buried, compounding the pandemic. The bishop of Carthage, a man named Cyprian, called out *The Parabalani*. They came and buried those bodies and they tended to the sick, helping to defeat the plague.

They were the risk takers.

They took care of the very people that were persecuting them. Because of their faith and love many Romans became believers. When their own loved ones abandoned them to die, it was the saints who loved them and brought them to healing, both physically and spiritually.

Jesus said, "Greater love hath no man than this, that a man lay down his life for a friend." What is God telling us to do with this plague that we face today? What does God want from us? Could it be that this is a time for a harvest of souls? Could it be that this is the reason why God allowed it? This doesn't mean that he *caused* it. But perhaps he allowed it for the harvest of souls. Because He can work all things for the good, according to His purpose.

Even leaders are mentioning God today. I heard even the President say, "if this thing leaves right away, it will be a blessing from God." He said it would be a miracle from God. Could it be that our leaders will realize that we need God?

God never wastes anything. God has a purpose. Could it be that this is a time for a harvest of souls that otherwise could not be reached? We can't be afraid for our own lives to the point that we are not willing to help someone else. Saints, this is a great hour for us! We must not miss it. Like the old song says, "Hide it under a bushel? NO! I'm gonna let it shine!" We are light. We are salt. If people can't hear the good news from us, then we are failing.

ave you noticed that when the news comes on at 5:00 or 6:00, they usually end the broadcast with a positive story? This started during the recession. NBC was the first to realize that people were tired of bad news. So, on Fridays they would end with a good and uplifting story. They realized that people liked it and they began doing it more and more. And now it just seems to be the new norm.

CBS noticed more people switching to NBC because it was more positive, and that became their format also. ABC noticed that CBS and NBC were attracting more and more of their viewers, so they decided to also share good news. Good news is attractive. Good news draws people in.

Saints, we have the ultimate good news! And just like people started turning the channel to see more good news, if we share the gospel with them, and just put it out there, many people will start tuning in to our good news!

1 Corinthians 15:50-53 says, "Now this I say, brethren, that flesh and blood cannot inherit the kingdom of God; neither doth corruption inherit incorruption. Behold, I shew you a mystery; we shall not all sleep, but we shall all be changed, in a moment, in the twinkling of an eye, at the last trump: for the trumpet shall sound, and the dead shall be raised incorruptible, and we shall be changed. For this corruptible must put on incorruption, and this mortal must put on immortality."

ONE MOMENT

There is a moment in everyone's life that changes everything. They call it a *defining moment*. When you look back on your life, can you think of a moment that changed your life? A moment that changed the way you think? This is one of those moments that should change people. But there is a moment that is greater than all of the other moments combined. In this age of coronavirus, with all the fear and uncertainty that comes with it, we must remember this: In the twinkling of an eye, He will change us.

We have what the world calls a *doomsday clock*. The closest we have ever been to doomsday has been 2 minutes. The doomsday clock has shown anywhere from 2 to 14 minutes since it started ticking back in the 1940s. This clock is based on what is going on in the world and how close the experts think we are to the world's destruction. It is now at 100 seconds. This is the lowest it has ever been, since 1947. It is lower than than it was on 9/11. It is lower than the atomic bomb.

It has never been this low.

According to this clock, we are literally a-minute-and-a-half from midnight. From destruction. There is no playbook for handling this. Before you finish reading this book there could be a shout and all of the saints will be gone. One moment. The word *moment* comes from the Greek word that means atom. An atom is the smallest unit of ordinary matter.

It is said that we blink our eyes 15,000 to 20,0000 times every day. So, every day God has 15,000 to 20,000 opportunities to take us out of here. Someone said that a twinkling of an eye is 1/64,000 of a second. An atom is so small that we cannot divide it. *Atom* means something that can't be divided. It can't be cut. It's the smallest unit man can even think of. In one moment, in a twinkling, the saints will be gone.

This time of crisis, when the world is struggling with the effects of COVID-19, is not the final chapter for us. It is just a comma. As the Devil continues to wreak havoc, God may decide, "I've seen my children go through enough." There are two trumpets. One of them is the victory trumpet. The victory shout. We will hear that shout of victory. God tells us that those who died before us are coming too. Your mama, your grandmama, your granddaddy, you papa, your great grandparents. God's not leaving them. And those of us who are still alive will be caught up in a moment.

As I said, we have had four coronavirus-like crisis over the last 2,000 years. But we've had three new ones over the last 30 years. Each sickness came from an animal. Man did not have the resistance to fight it off. So, there is no playbook for this. But God tells us that there is a moment that is coming when we will no longer have to live in a world of such things. He will take us out of this world in a moment.

We will be caught up.

Have you been baptized? Have you given your life to Christ? Is He your Lord? Remember I told you that during the Spanish flu people died in their buggies on their way to the hospital. People died in the waiting room. If it is your time, nothing can save you. All the *Charmin* toilet paper in the world cannot protect you. So, this is a time to make sure that you are ready, and a time to make sure that you *stay* ready, so when Jesus comes you will *be* ready.

I have another acronym for coronavirus. **Can't Overtake, Relegate, Obliterate, Negate, Annihilate, Viscerate,**

Intimidate, Relegate Us Saints. This virus can't defeat us. We have the victory.

Ventilators do not offer a cure. We still need an antibody. We still need the medicine. And we have access to an eternal ventilator and eternal resuscitation. I have been saved. I have been redeemed. Saints—be of good cheer. Don't be frightened. Don't be afraid. Stay close with one another. Stay in communication with each other. Pray for each other. Encourage one another. Read God's Word.

Trust God that He will make a way!

CHAPTER ELEVEN

"This wasn't supposed to happen"

IN EARLY 2020, the Dow Jones Industrial Average was at the highest point in its history, and it appeared to be unstoppable. People were enjoying high returns on their retirement funds, 401k's, and stock portfolios. Everyone seemed to be making money. Businesses were raising salaries because they could not find enough people to work. Businesses, big and small, were hiring, but positions went unfilled. For example, *Taco Bell* was finding it hard to find managers until they decided to initiate a program where they would be paid $100,000 per year.

Things were that good.

In the political world, as the primaries got up and running, the focus was on whether Bernie or Biden would win the Democratic nomination, the impeachment of Donald Trump, and the question of whether or not there would be a female vice presidential nominee. There were skirmishes and tensions in Iran and Iraq, while some Americans found reason to rejoice as our troops in Afghanistan started to come home.

And on the other side of the world in China they were battling a new virus, something called COVID-19. But that was far away and few noticed. We felt safe. What little we knew just convinced us to shake our heads—they should have known better than to have illegal seafood and exotic wildlife shops. Eating that stuff was dangerous. So, we didn't feel too bad for them, even when the virus shut down a city the size of Chicago. No alarms went off here at home. After all, China was an 18-hour flight away.

No big deal.

Then, all of a sudden, everything changed. We were blindsided. It was like an asteroid had struck. Strange things started happening, and then it all started snowballing. Quickly, our world began to look very different. College students were now at home taking lessons via computer or working from home. Students put in so much effort and work and they just knew it would be worth it when they graduated but many of them are not able to find jobs.

People planned weddings, spending $10,000 to $20,000 on what they hoped would be a magical day, where they would be surrounded by hundreds of their friends and family, only to be told that they could only have 10 people attend. *This wasn't supposed to happen.*

We all had plans, aspirations, and dreams. Vacations we planned and saved for have been cancelled. Businesses we have poured our sweat and tears into building have been closed, and employees laid off.

This wasn't supposed to happen.

Physicians who have spent 12 years of their lives in school so that they can save lives are now in danger of losing their own.

This wasn't supposed to happen.

Prince Charles got COVID-19. Boris Johnson, the British Prime Minister got COVID-19. Athletes and celebrities got COVID-19. No playoffs, no hockey, no *March Madness*, no basketball. We are shuttered in our homes, struggling to find ways to pass the time. I mean, how many times *can* we read Psalm 23?

This wasn't supposed to happen.

We have discovered a concept called *social distancing*. We have to limit our numbers in gatherings. We have to stay six feet apart. Even funerals and wakes can only allow 10 people at any time. Memorial services have to be live streamed on the Internet. Are we living in a nightmare? Can someone wake me up? Pinch me?

This wasn't supposed to happen.

Cities have been shut down. Policemen are on the borders, preventing people from coming in or going out. There are shortages of masks, gowns—and doctors. Churches are not allowed to gather in person. Everyone is shut in their homes. The world has been turned upside down, and the greatest nation in the history of mankind, with the greatest number of so-called believers, has been caught off guard.

This wasn't supposed to happen.

Now, there are *some* good things happening. Prison doors are swinging open. People who have been incarcerated for just smoking a joint, even though million-dollar embezzlers still walk free, are finally being released. Landlords are offering rent forgiveness. People are helping each other. But at the heart of it we are all screaming:

"This wasn't supposed to happen!"

I am grateful that I have the opportunity to livestream my sermons, but many pastors do not have this available to them. They can't talk to their people and shepherd them during these difficult days. It is not the way they saw things happening. Not the way they had written the script. They had it all planned out. They were being intentional.

This wasn't supposed to happen.

When we cry out to God in our times of trouble, the ancient prophet Elijah comes to my mind. He had to learn how to move from the natural to the supernatural. He had to learn how to trust what he could not see. He was the first individual who experienced social distancing. And He had a great meal plan—food was flown in by a raven.

That's even better than *Grubhub*.

We are not the first generation on earth to have problems. Trouble has always been around.

Elijah may be a prophet for our times.

CHAPTER TWELVE

"God always has a there for you"

"And Elijah the Tishbite, who was of the inhabitants of
Gilead, said unto Ahab, As the Lord God of Israel liveth,
before whom I stand, there shall not be dew nor rain these
years, but according to my word. And the word of the
Lord came unto him, saying, Get thee hence, and turn
thee eastward, and hide thyself by the brook Cherith, that
is before Jordan. And it shall be, that thou shalt drink of
the brook; and I have commanded the ravens to feed thee
there." —Kings 17:1-4

AND SO, GOD invented social distancing.

If we could ask Elijah for his thoughts about our current troubles, he might say: "Well, the first thing I had to do was distance myself from everyone else and trust God. I had to trust God for my meals. Sometimes the food was what I liked. Sometimes it wasn't. But it always met the need."

God sent Elijah to Cherith, a place that literally meant *cutting place*. God sometimes tells us that there is some cutting He must do. During this pandemic, part of God's plan is to cut. He is cutting off some of the distractions, idols, and chains that have complicated our lives. These things have hindered us doing what God has called us to do. Everybody is going to have their Cherith, or cutting place. What makes this time in our lives so remarkable is that everyone is residing in Cherith at the same time, in the same place, and God is uniquely cutting and shaping each of us.

A few verses later it says, *"And it came to pass after a while, that the brook dried up, because there had been no rain in the land. And the word of the Lord came unto him, saying, Arise, get thee to Zarephath, which belongeth to Zidon, and dwell there: behold, I have commanded a widow woman there to sustain thee."*

The brook dried up, and the ravens stopped coming.

But Elijah did not get upset.

We have to realize that where and who we are is very important to God. The only way we can hold God to His promises is if we are where He wants us to be. We have to be *there*. If God's blessings for you are in St. Louis, you can't be in Houston.

"The raven shall feed thee there. I've commanded a widow there to sustain thee." God always has a *there* for you. Even though many of us feel stuck in our homes right now, God is telling us that we are in the right place at the right time and that He can take care of us *there*.

God directed the man of God. Elijah had already been humiliated and embarrassed by having a raven feed him, and then God told him to go to the neediest person in Zarephath. Zarephath was the headquarters of Baal. This is where Baal worship was supreme. I find that very interesting. God sent Elijah to the enemy's camp and told him that He would take care of him there. Now if you don't know your map, Zarephath was 100 miles away. Cherith was in what is now the Kingdom of Jordan. Zarephath is in what is now Southern Lebanon. Zidon was the region.

That's Jezebel's hometown.

Queen Jezebel was the personification of evil. She became a persistent metaphor for evil later in scripture and still holds that distinction to this day. Born in Phoenicia, she was completely immersed in its pagan culture and its gods. Under her influence, there developed a syncretic mishmash of religious ideas that became widespread in the culture. And Zidon became a center for Baal worship.

You want me to go where?

God wanted him to go out in plain sight, cross over no-man's land, and be totally exposed to any and all potential risks. Now implicit in the promise was, "Go there—I will protect you." *I guess I'm going to get there, so I guess I shouldn't worry about this.*

But I'm sure he was at least a little nervous.

Zarephath means refining. God was saying that after He cuts away the things that are hindering us from living our best life, He then refines us. He is after something. Sometimes we get impatient with God and say, "I need the Lord to speak to me right *now*." During the COVID-19 crisis, we long for God to speak to us. But sometimes, more important than God speaking *to* you, is God speaking *over* you. God told Elijah that He spoke with authority. He **commanded**. Why is that so important? Because the word has the power to create cosmos out of chaos and draw order out of disorder. The word has the power to separate light from darkness. The word has the power to bless, produce, create, and protect.

And God tells us, "I have spoken over you. I have commanded somebody to watch over you. Be assured that if my name is on your house and if my blood is covering you, I am taking care of you." It may be with angels. It may be with a widow. It may be a raven. It may be the president. But God says, "I have commanded, spoken with authority over your life, and it is going to be all right."

Elijah went to the widow's house. She was most likely a young single mother, probably a widow in her 20s. She believed that she and her son were near death. She was prepared to die. She got the last bit of oil and the last meal. Her plan was to prepare the bread for her and her son, and when they ate their last meal they would die. But Elijah approached her and asked her to make him a meal *first*.

"There is no way I'm feeding you."

But Elijah said, *"Fear not; go and do as thou hast said: but make me thereof a little cake first, and bring it unto me, and after make for thee and for thy son. For thus saith the Lord God of Israel, the barrel of meal shall not waste, neither shall the cruse of oil fail, until the day that the Lord sendeth rain upon the earth."*

So, the widow did as he said. She obeyed what was spoken, because God had already spoken over the situation. She thought that she was getting ready to die, but what she didn't know was that God had overruled death. God was overshadowing death.

Death had no power to destroy her.

CHAPTER THIRTEEN

"The Perplexity of God"

MANY OF US are worried about COVID-19, but we must remember what God has already done in our lives. The fact that we are still here is a testimony to the fact that God has already spoken over us. That is why you haven't lost your mind during this pandemic. Because death has no power to destroy us. When the storms come, we don't drown. When our resources are low, we still don't run out. When we lose a job, God still provides. When we go through the fire, it doesn't burn us and we don't even smell like smoke. Because God had already spoken over us.

Be encouraged, if you feel terrorized by COVID-19—God has *already* spoken over you.

Many of us are worried about supplies and resources. We are worried about finances, so we are watching the *Dow* and the *S&P*. But we must remember that wealth is determined by promise. We would do better to stop looking at the *Dow* and instead tap into the Divine Owner's Wealth. God is our *S&P*. He is our safety. He is our protection. He is our source. He is our provider. Wealth is tied to promise, and God has given us a promise—"I will take care of you."

Time went by and Elijah became a part of the widow's family. I like to imagine that he played ball with her son. Maybe they had chased each other. I like to think that maybe Elijah and the boy had funny nicknames for each other. So, after all of that social distancing, with only the ravens for comfort, Elijah finally had a family, and he felt good about it. Life was looking better.

This reminds me of what happened with us in early 2020. Everything was lining up just the way we wanted it. We were feeling pretty comfortable. Everything was going according to the way God had planned it, but something happened. Something blindsided us. Muhammad Ali once said that it is not the hardest punch that knocks you down, it's the punch that you didn't see coming. We did not see COVID-19 coming.

And Elijah did not see what was coming next.

In verse 17, we read, *"And it came to pass after these things, that the son of the woman, the mistress of the house, fell sick; and his sickness was so sore, that there was no breath left in him."* Theologians believe that there was some type of virus that attacked him rapidly, to the point where he could not breathe anymore. It hit suddenly and rapidly.

Sound familiar?

The virus took a healthy young boy and rapidly destroyed his life to the point where he could not breathe. There were no oxygen tanks in those days. No ventilators. No respiratory therapists. There was no one to help him. This young boy died quickly because something had attacked his respiratory system.

And he died.

Verse 18 says, *"And she said unto Elijah, 'What have I to do with thee, O thou man of God? Art thou come unto me to call my sin to remembrance and to slay my son'?"* The widow likely thought, just like so many of us when bad things happen, "God must be punishing me. I must have done something wrong." One of the most puzzling and frustrating things in life is when bad things come into our lives while we are trying to do everything right.

The widow must have thought, "I'm taking care of the man of God. I'm in God's will. I'm being obedient to God and everything else, and despite all of this, something terrible is happening." Our first resort in times like these is to rely on our power of *reason*. This is called the *perplexity of God.* The widow does not understand what is going on. C.S. Lewis said that pain is God's megaphone, when he cannot get our attention any other way.

The widow might have thought, "This is not what I expected. This should not be happening. This is not what I thought would take place. *This was not supposed to happen.* I gave the man of God my last meal. I put a roof over his head. We were supposed to be safe and provided for. This should have been the safest house in Zarephath."

And we say the same thing today. *This was not supposed to happen.* Not in the United States. Maybe it could happen in an atheistic country like China, but not here in America.

When I preach in my church, I'm not supposed to be preaching to just a few people in the building while everyone else is live streaming. I'm not supposed to be social distancing and unable to get close to anyone. I'm not supposed to be wearing a mask and gloves and wiping and spraying everything down. I'm not supposed to be afraid every time someone sneezes or coughs.

This was not in my script for 2020. This year was supposed to be a year of vision—a 20/20 vision. This was supposed to be a year of "name it and claim it." This was to be a year of "gab it and grab it." It was supposed to be a year when I would finally get what I was believing God for. No, no, no.

This was not supposed to happen.

What we understand is that even ministry has rocked us to the point where we believe that somehow we can have a relationship with God in which we live in one eternal bliss. During the process of serving God, to whatever extent we attempt, we will become wealthy and everything will just fall into place the way we dreamed it would. But that isn't what happened. Instead, we went from *gratitude* to *grasping*. We went from gratitude to trying to gather. Even with social distancing there is a risk in any type of gathering. And many of us are living in fear, so much that we can't help anyone.

We are barely living.

We are in a time and place where life has been turned upside down. We live in a world that is full of sin caused by Adam and Eve. They ushered in diseases, infection, viruses, and everything else.

The widow certainly felt this way. She forgot about what God had already done. But Elijah didn't. He didn't defend himself. He didn't try to explain. He didn't say, "I know. My bad. I know I gave you a promise and now I'm embarrassed and humiliated." Elijah doesn't say anything to defend himself. Even though this horrible tragedy happened on his watch. He had promised the woman that they would be fine. The son was not *supposed to* die.

But even in that moment, Elijah was willing to trust God.

It's funny how sometimes you don't see the obvious thing coming. You think you know what life has in store for you. You think you're prepared. You think you can handle it and then Boom like a Thunderclap—Something comes at you out of nowhere and catch you off guard.

CYNTHIA HAND

CHAPTER FOURTEEN

"Unchartered territory"

ARE WE WILLING to trust God the same way we trusted Him when our jobs were secure? The same way we trusted Him when everything was going well and things were falling perfectly into place? Are we willing, now, to trust Him the same way? How's your level of faith? Check your faith gauge? Are you running on empty?

Elijah responded to the widow, *"Give me thy son. And he took him out of her bosom, and carried him up into the loft, where he abode, and laid him upon his own bed."* The fact that she gave Elijah her son indicates that she still had a measure of faith.

Elijah was probably every bit as perplexed as the widow. He was just as confused. He didn't know why it was happening, either.

This was early on in his prophetic journey. Up until this point, the only thing he had done was go before Ahab and Jezebel to say, "It's going to rain." The second thing he did was tell the widow, "Give me a cake first, and then God will take care of you." So far, that was it.

The fiery stuff would come later.

There comes a time in a life of faith when it is time to move to the next level. There comes a point when you either pray or panic. Elijah was at this point. He realized that he was stretched to do something he had never done before. He had to choose to believe God for the miraculous. He didn't argue. He didn't complain. He didn't say, "Why me?" He brought the little boy into his secret closet, to his own bed. Why? Because that is where he met God every day. That is where he had fellowship with the Almighty. That is where he prayed. That is where he did his knee work—where he called on God.

What we learn from Elijah is that crisis is not what makes a leader. It only reveals what is in you. When a crisis comes, you can't all of a sudden say, "God make me a great spiritual leader." No. A crisis will only squeeze out of you what is in you. If you squeeze an orange, you won't get apple juice. If you squeeze a grapefruit you won't get orange juice.

Many are afraid today. There are many who are suffering from anxiety. People start to believe that COVID-19 is bigger that Jesus. But in the midst of all of these fearful people, there are people of faith who have been prepared by a relationship with God who will rise up and tell the Devil, "This means war!"

That was Elijah's position. He would not bow down to an idol. An idol is anything that we put before God. COVID-19 is, in a very real sense, an idol that many are bowing before. They worship the great COVID-19. They are terrorized by it. They can't sleep. They can't eat. They can't pray because COVID-19.

That idol must fall.

Too many have already been defeated on the battlefield of faith. We can't afford to lose many more. Too many preachers, teachers, and mighty men and women of God have already surrendered, and they are content to just sit and wait for dooms day.

Instead, we must pray until victory comes.

I serve the God of my past, the God of my future, and the God of my present. He is the same yesterday, today, and forever. God is still able to do something that will blow our minds. God is still able to do the unexplainable, undeniable, incredible, and astounding. God is still able to work miracles in our lives.

Elijah may have been disappointed. But he trusted God. He may have been perplexed. But he trusted God. He didn't have the answer. He was confused, blindsided, and unprepared. The widow's son's death was not part of the plan. But he trusted God. Why? Because he had been to Cherith (cutting) and at Zarephath (shaping, refining.)

How does one build great faith? It's not when the crisis comes, but rather it is a daily effort. Jesus must be the center of our lives every day. We pray, "Give us this day our daily bread." Faith is an everyday practice. Communion with God is every day. Obeying God is every day. Saying that God is number one is every day. You see, it is our faithfulness in the little things that prepare us for the big things. COVID-19 is a big thing. It is a deadly thing. It is a destructive thing. It is a demonic thing. But it can be vanquished by great faith.

God says to the church, the body of Christ, "Take charge." God is telling us to pull out the heavy artillery. He is telling us that we are not thermometers—we are thermostats. A thermometer only measures the temperature. It simply records and reflects the temperature. And that is all that is happening around us. We look to the news media, and we are just reflecting, recording, and reporting. And as the number of

COVID-19 cases rises, we get more and more discouraged. But God tells us that we are His children.

We are, instead, spiritual *thermostats*. In other words, if it is too hot, we can change the temperature. If COVID-19 has us anxious and fearful, we can adjust the thermostat. How do we adjust the spiritual thermostat?

We pray.

Elijah was a man of prayer. He prayed at Cherith. He prayed at Zarephath, and the Bible tells us that he lifted up the young boy. He took him to the other room and he started praying. Listen to how Elijah prayed. *"And he cried unto the Lord, and said, O Lord my God, hast thou also brought evil upon the widow with whom I sojourn, by slaying her son?"* In other words, Elijah prayed what she was saying. He literally was crying out to God, saying "Lord, please listen to what the widow is saying. She doesn't have a husband to take care of her. There is no social security. There is no disability. There is no life insurance. There is no welfare. Her son is the key to her survival. God, without him she will die. God, what the widow is saying is that she is hurt. She is confused. She is in pain. She thought you brought this on because you didn't love her. She thought you were punishing her."

He went to the Lord in prayer. That was his weapon. And that is our weapon today. Are you worried about COVID-19?

Pray. The fastest way to stop this virus, the quickest way to slow it down, will be the prayers of the righteous.

Psalm 107, simply says, *"Lord, help us."* This is the starting point, but not the end. We need to start praying, and then we need to *keep on* praying. The Bible says that Elijah prayed three times. If God doesn't answer the first time, don't give up.

It just means that you are in uncharted territory.

CHAPTER FIFTEEN

"It's time to stretch"

MANY OF OUR prayers are over small things. But now, we are praying for something so much bigger. Just like Elijah. He knew it was time to bring his prayers and his faith to the next level. It was time to change the thermostat. Before that moment, there was no record in the Bible of the kind of faith he needed in that moment. His faith had to be stretched. He couldn't pray the same prayer he had always prayed. It had to be an agonizing prayer. A travailing prayer.

It had to be *warfare* prayer.

This is the kind of prayer that God wants now from His church. He wants us to go to war in prayer. We have to stretch ourselves. We have to pray until we get an answer. We have to pray until there is deliverance. We have to pray until COVID-19 loses its power. We have to pray until the virus dies.

It takes persistent prayer. It takes a push to pray until something happens. Until we have a breakthrough. Until we can terrorize hell instead of allowing hell to terrorize us. Until we kill the virus instead of the virus killing us. We pray until we turn the arrow around. We pray until the life and the potency and the power of COVID-19 dies.

God is saying to the Body of Christ, "It's time to stretch." Just like Elijah, we are in uncharted waters. Pastors are trying to figure out how to keep ministry going when there isn't much money coming in. The government is trying to figure out the best way to defeat this virus and protect and serve its people through things like mandating masks and printing stimulus checks. All of this will help, but the real battle is *spiritual*.

The virus is demonic. It flies in the air. It is anonymous. It shows up, regardless of precautions. Nobody knows where it came from or who got it. But we know the truth. Greater is He that is in us than he that is in the world. If God is for us, who can be against us?

So, Elijah prayed.

And God wants all believers to be praying in these times. COVID-19 will not destroy us if we pray. COVID-19 will not linger as long as it wants to linger if we pray. COVID-19 will not stop until we pray. Just because we are saints does not mean that COVID-19 can't hit us. COVID-19 is no respecter of persons. We have to pray, and, as we pray, we are going to see God move.

How long did Elijah pray? We don't know. But we do know that he didn't stop praying until he got a breakthrough and the boy came to life. *"And the Lord heard the voice of Elijah..."* That also means that he heard the tone of Elijah's voice. It was not just repetition. It was not just a nice, pretty prayer. God heard the tone of Elijah's voice and the desperation. God could feel what Elijah was feeling, because Elijah was feeling what the woman was feeling.

The widow's feelings were transferred to Elijah, and then Elijah took those feelings to God. He then added *his* feelings of being perplexed and baffled. God heard the tone. He heard the pleading. The Lord heard his cry. In other words, it was not a quick, five-minute prayer, like we often pray. It was agonizing. He was praying and crying. He was crying and praying. And the Bible tells us, "Weeping may endure for a night, but joy comes in the morning."

"And the woman said to Elijah, now by this I know thou art a man of God, and that the word of the Lord in thy mouth is truth."

That's it. God is telling us that when we get that, COVID-19 will die. God is saying that it's not a punishment, it's perfection. Zarephath is refining. God knew that Elijah would have to one day face down all of the prophets of Baal, so his faith had to be refined and stretched. He had to move from believing that a raven could bring him dinner, to believing he could ask God to raise the dead.

He had to have a greater faith for what was ahead of him.

God is telling his believers today that we have to have greater faith for what's ahead of us. One of the things I know in the Spirit is that COVID-19 is not the last one. We have entered the beginning of the end times and these things will become more and more frequent. I do not mean this to terrorize anyone. I am just speaking the truth. We must be prepared. God is telling us we need to get to the point that we realize nothing is as strong and as powerful as God. He is more precious than gold and silver. We need Him. God's specialty has always been to get us to know him, and when we don't make that a priority, then God will allow things to happen to try to get us back in line, so that we can get to know Him.

God wants our faith to be stronger than it is right now. He wants our prayer lives to be richer than they are right now. He wants our hopes to be fortified and our testimonies more powerful. God is saying, "I'm not looking for people with religion, I'm looking for people with a relationship."

When Michael Jordan played basketball, there was something known as "the Jordan rule." If Michael had the ball, put as many players as possible on him. If Michael ran by you without the ball, hit him. Whoever Michael was guarding, give him the ball so it will wear him down trying to guard that person. Players were told to bump him. Hit him. Whatever it took. And then in the last two minutes of the game players were told to intensify the Jordan rule. In those final moments it didn't matter if Jordan was losing, because if he got the ball, even in the last few moments of the game, he had the ability to do some amazing things that could move his team from loser to winner.

We have to apply the Jordan rule to our prayer life. There are two minutes left, but God is telling the body of Christ to keep our eyes on Jesus. God is ready to do something that is amazing and we don't want to miss it. God wants us to keep praying. Keep fasting. Keep believing.

As Albertina Walker said:

Makes no difference what the problem,
(I can go to God in prayer).
Yes, I have this blessed assurance,
(I can go to God in prayer).

He will take my gloom and sorrow,
(Turn it into light).
He will comfort, strengthen, and keep me,
(I can go to God in prayer).

I can call him when I need him,
Our Father, up in heaven;
I can go to God in prayer.

Sometimes my burdens they get so heavy,
(I can go to God in prayer).
I have found one who is so faithful,
(I can go to God in prayer).
He will take my gloom and sadness,
(Turn it into light).
He will never, ever forsake me
(I can go to God in prayer).

CHAPTER SIXTEEN

"The Way to Is Through"

COVID-19 HAS CHANGED the world. COVID-19 has changed the very fabric of society. COVID-19 has even changed churches. And we know that once things get back to normal, the church will have changed permanently. There are some things about the church that will never be the same again. Now, some of this has been good, because as pastors, we've learned we can minister without praise dancers, banners, or orchestras.

We've learned that the Word has a life of its own.

One of the things I've been hearing a lot is a question: "Will church attendance still be as important as it used to be?" Frankly, there are some who believe we are moving into an era where church attendance will not be as important as it used to be. Time will tell, I suppose. Some note that we have online church now, and there are more people online than in the actual pews. Some even suggest that many of the big "multi-site" churches will probably have to revisit their strategy, because now there will be more people online who may think, "Now I don't have to go to one of the multi-site locations. I can get everything online."

So, things have definitely changed for the church.

There probably won't be any more stand and greet. There probably won't be any more holy hugs, at least for a while, unless it's your relative or your husband or your wife. Bagels are out. Doughnuts, too. They may still have the coffee. I don't know. Getting rid of coffee might be too radical. But handshakes will definitely be out. It's far from an automatic given that folks will be coming to church the way they used to.

I read an article recently, and in it this gentleman made an important point. Many churches now have more viewers than they used to have in actual attendance. It's nothing for pastors to say, "We have two times, three times, four times, five times as many now online as we had in church."

A lot of pastors and church leaders have gotten excited about that. "Do we really need to go back to the sanctuary? We have so many viewers. Do we really need to go back to what we used to do?" But in the article, the writer says we cannot use online as the new ministry metric. It caught my attention. He said measuring the success of your church by the number in attendance is weak.

Many times, people say, "Well, we have 6,000. We have 5,000. We have 220,000. We have three million." But that 80/20 percent rule still applies. It's weak to measure your church effectiveness by attendance, and it's even weaker to measure it by eyeballs on a computer screen. You have a better chance of people being focused when they're actually in the house of the Lord.

The writer said, "Pastors and leaders, don't fool yourselves. People may have you online. They're cooking. They're cleaning. They're talking. If they don't like what you're saying, they're not engaged. Don't think that every time you're on, everybody is sitting mesmerized in front of their screens listening to every word you say. They're not. There's a whole lot of distraction going on."

It takes 30 days to break a habit, and it takes 30 days to develop a habit. Church attendance had been declining before

COVID-19. What's happening now is that a lot of the folks on the fence have now either decided, "I don't think I really need church at all" or "I can just get it on the Internet." Online church is not going anywhere. It is a great tool, but what we have to understand is that we cannot measure our effectiveness by how many folks are online during C0VID-19.

Will attendance still be as important? My answer is *yes*. One writer suggests that people who are used to going to church will come back to church. David said, "I was glad, I was excited, I was overcome with joy when they said…" *They* are the saints, the church. "Let us go to the house of the Lord." Church will always be important. Coming together will always be important, and nothing can replace that.

Jesus said the gates of hell shall not prevail against the church. The writer of the Book of Hebrews said, "Forsake not the assembling of yourselves together." The church is a preaching, teaching, praying, and worshiping organism. It works most effectively when those who are part of the church can come together in one a place, wherever it may be, to worship, to pray, to study God's Word, and most of all, to praise and worship God.

There will always be a church.

There will always be church buildings.

There will always be some place I can physically go and worship and praise my God. We're not getting rid of online.

It's here. But Zoom will never replace the church. Teleconferencing will not replace coming together in church. Online streaming will never replace coming together in church.

Even President Trump said, "The church doors need to be open." He said the church has not been treated fairly. He said, "We need more prayer." He said the church affects the psyche of the nation. When God can have the President stand up and say, "Open the doors of the church. If the governors don't do it, I will do it," it means the church doors must be open.

Online streaming is great. It's not going anywhere. We're going to look at ways to improve it. We're going to look at ways to get better. But what I hear God saying is that nothing will ever replace the church, we who make up the church, coming together in whatever facility is our place of worship. Nothing will ever replace the coming together of the saints of God to praise and worship.

CHAPTER SEVENTEEN

"Journey back to the house of the Lord"

"How amiable are thy tabernacles, O Lord of hosts! My soul longeth, yea, even fainteth for the courts of the Lord: my heart and my flesh crieth out for the living God. Yea, the sparrow hath found an house, and the swallow a nest for herself, where she may lay her young, even thine altars, O Lord of hosts, my King, and my God. Blessed are they that dwell in thy house: they will be still praising thee. Selah. Blessed is the man whose strength is in thee; in whose heart are the ways of them. Who passing through the valley of Baca make it a well; the rain also

filleth the pools. They go from strength to strength, every one of them in Zion appeareth before God." —Psalm 84

SOME SAY PSALM 84 was written by Jehoshaphat. Some say it was written by the sons of Korah. But most say it was written by David. He wrote about the journey to get to Jerusalem. To get to Zion. To get to *church*. He tells the tale of the journey to get back to the house of the Lord.

The first verse of the Psalm reads, *"How amiable are thy tabernacles, O Lord of hosts!"* Amiable means lovely or desirable. The writer was looking back at past experiences that he had at church. He was not just an occasional visitor like we have these days. You know the types—the people who come on Christmas, Easter, and Mother's Day. This was someone who was looking back through the lens of his heart and the eyes of his soul. He was remembering when God's people were gathered together and when the saints of God were all in one place. When there was praise and worship being lifted to the Most High. People were shouting. People were lifting their hands. People were dancing. People were proclaiming, "God is good all the time, and all the time God is good!" People were shouting "AMEN" and "HALLELUJAH."

When he was talking about how amiable, delightful and lovely the tabernacle, it was during a period of time before Solomon's temple had been built. So, he was not talking about the extraordinary beauty on the outside. He was not talking about the gold and the brass. No. He was talking about what happened on the *inside*, when God's people came together to worship Him and lift Him up.

In this first verse we can see that the Psalmist remembers what many of us may have already forgotten. He remembered going to church. He remembered when times were hard, he went to church and his spirit was renewed. He remembered the times when he thought no one cared, so he went to church and encountered the unconditional love of God. He remembered the time when he felt like he was a nobody and was going nowhere fast, so he went to church and was reminded that he was a child of God. He remembered the time when he was sick and he went to church where the people prayed for him and laid hands on him and he was healed of his sickness. He remembered a word that was spoken. A song that had touched his heart. He remembered how important the church was to him.

One of the greatest, most precious sights on earth is when the saints of God come together for church.

The Psalmist goes on to say, *"My soul longeth, yea, even fainteth for the courts of the Lord: my heart and my flesh crieth out for the living God."* He is crying out because he is suffering and is longing for those days in the tabernacle. Because, even when he simply thought about those times, his heart quickened, and His eyes began to brighten up.

If the author was David, then we can understand it, because David said, *"There's only one thing I desire, that I may dwell in the house of the Lord forever."* In 1 Chronicles 29:3, he said, *"I set my affection to the house of the Lord."* In other words, David loved being in church. He longed to be in church. He ached to be in church. This is the language of a lover who is lovesick. That feeling that you get when you love someone who is no longer in your life. You simply long to be with that person. David is describing a holy lovesickness for the courts of the Lord, to be in the house of God with the saints of God.

David is expressing the need to be in the house of the Lord, and in the presence of God. He was struggling with life because he was far away from the tabernacle. He needed to get back to the fellowship with his brothers and sisters. He desired to return to the place where the glory of God is manifested and His name is on the door. David was so weak with this desire that he felt like fainting. The word, fainting, means to be consumed with longing. He was consumed 24/7 and 365 days a year. He knew that he had a lot of information, but what he really needed was inspiration. And inspiration comes from the Word of God and the gathering together with other believers who were on the journey with him.

Verse three says, *"Yea, the sparrow hath found an house, and the swallow a nest for herself..."* It is amazing sometimes, when you are going through something hard, what you can become envious about. This is David. But David wasn't jealous of the people living in fine houses. He wasn't envious of people with the newest gadget or the latest model Mercedes Benz. He was jealous of a sparrow. Why?

Because they found a place.

The sparrow is one of the least important creatures on earth. Jesus said that you can buy two of them for a penny. In other words, a sparrow was cheaper than a goldfish. A sparrow was unimportant and insignificant, but he had found a place in the house of the Lord. So, David was envious of the sparrow.

He was envious of the swallow. The swallow was a wanderer. The sparrow would stay at its place for the length of its life. But the swallow would wander. It was a busy bird. It would fly from one place to another. It would show up in seasons and then go away.

David was saying that even those people who do not go to the tabernacle on a regular basis somehow or another made it to the house of the Lord, yet he was stuck outside of God's house, desiring to be there.

David is saying that even the unwanted can find a home at church. It is harder for the unwanted to watch a live stream and find deliverance, than it is to physically join together with the body of believers. Wherever we gather together, whether it is in a traditional church building or somewhere else, it is a place where the needy can come and find a place of shelter. The uninvited can come and find what they are looking for. David tells us to look at the sparrow. Nobody invited the sparrow, but the sparrow came anyway because he was needy. The sparrow cannot offer anything. Instead, he needs provision. He came to the church and he found it.

The church represents a permanent dwelling. First, David talked about the sparrow. The sparrow found a home there. Not a hotel. Not an Airbnb. He found a home. A church is a place where you can establish roots. It is a place where you can find people to love and who love you. A church is a place where we can dwell from generation to generation.

Next, David talked about the swallow. The swallow found a nest for herself, a place to rest. She found a nest where she could lay her young. She not only found a place to get fed, to find shelter, to be safe, but she also found a place where she could make her nest and raise her children.

Our children need to be in church. There is so much going on in their lives right now. So much change. So much craziness in the media that they are being exposed to. So much hate in this world. Things that are being taught that aren't biblical. In fact, a rising number of preachers are proclaiming false things that are not theologically correct.

And a lot of people are soaking it in.

CHAPTER EIGHTEEN

"We can't escape the valley"

THERE ARE SOME amazing preachers out there, but there are also false prophets, those who twist the Word of God. That's why it is so important to have a church home. So, when these winds of false doctrine come our way, we won't be swayed.

And He Himself gave some to be apostles, some prophets, some evangelists, and some pastors and teachers, for the equipping of the saints for the work of ministry, for the edifying of the body of Christ, till we all come to the unity of the faith and of the knowledge of the Son of God, to a perfect man, to the measure of the stature of the fullness of Christ; that we should no longer be children, tossed to and fro and carried about with every wind of doctrine, by the trickery of men, in the cunning craftiness of deceitful plotting, but, speaking the truth in love, may grow up in all things into Him who is the head— Christ—Ephesians 4:11-15 (NKJV)

We have to have a house, a tabernacle, where not only can we find rest for our souls, not only where we can find safety and shelter, but where our kids can grow in the nurture and admonition of the Lord. So, our kids can be trained and can be imparted with the Word of God.

I need a church. You need a church. I need a tabernacle. You need a tabernacle. I need a temple. You need a temple. We all must make our way back to the tabernacle of the Lord of hosts.

Have you ever been jealous of a bird? David was jealous and envious of the birds because they were at church. They were safe. Their kids were safe from the bombardment of the world around them.

Verse four says, *"Blessed are they that dwell in thy house: they will be still praising thee."* Those who dwell in the house of the

Lord are going to praise God regardless of what is going on around them. They will never stop praising Him.

Verse five says, *"Blessed is the man whose strength is in thee; in whose heart are the ways of them."* In other words, if God is with you, and He is your number one priority, and the source of your strength, then you are a blessed man. We are blessed when our hearts pursue God. When our hearts are obedient to God. When our hearts are committed to God. When our hearts lean on God. When our hearts long to know the will and the ways of God. When our hearts are not satisfied until we know that we have given our all to Him. When our hearts are postured in this way, God promises to strengthen us and to do a new work in us.

Verse six says, *"Who passing through the valley of Baca make it a well; the rain also filleth the pools."* There is no doubt that we have been in a valley. The whole world has been in a valley. Everyone who has breath has been in a valley during this time of pandemic.

But we also each have our own personal valleys that we walk through. Valleys are deep places. Valleys are scary places. Valleys are dry places. Valleys are depressed places. Valleys are discouraging places. Valleys are perplexing places. Valleys are frustrating places. In order to get to the other side, to the place where God wants us to be, we have to go through the valley.

The way *to* is *through.*

The author of this Psalm understood this. In order to get back to the house of God he had to go through the valley. The way to is through. We can't escape the valley. We have all faced pain. We have all dealt with sorrow and grief. We have all experienced disappointment. We have all faced scary times filled with worry and dread. We have all been in dry places. We have felt like we were about to faint, and that we didn't have the strength to go on. David had highs and lows. If there is anyone who understands what it is like to go through a valley it is David. He has been there. He understands what we are going through and dealing with.

Nobody wants to stay in the valley. The greatest danger in the valley is losing your perspective. Too often, in the valley we are reactive instead of proactive. We are driven by our emotions and feelings, instead of by a sound mind. And because of this, many of us fall down and stay in the valley. Too many of us accept the valley as our destination and quit. Many of us have pitched tents in the valley. Many of us have parked in the valley. We have made homes in the valley. Some have even died in the valley. We aren't supposed to stay there. We are not supposed to die there. Sometimes we are stopped there for a time, but we have to keep the perspective of knowing where we are headed.

Have you ever been somewhere in your car and seen a sign that said *Temporary Parking*? You can only park between the hours of 8:00 and 5:00 on Mondays and Thursdays. But if you park any other day, or after 5:00, you will get a ticket. There is a consequence. Every valley is like temporary parking. God doesn't want us to rest for too long in the valley. He doesn't want us to lie down for too long in the valley. God doesn't want us to get too comfortable in the valley. Because our destination is Zion. We must get to Jerusalem.

We must get to church.

COVID-19 is a valley. Your trial or test that you are going through is a valley. Make sure you don't forget your destination. You are simply passing through this hard time. It is something you have to go through to get to the other side. You couldn't escape it. You couldn't get around it. But you can't stop there.

You must keep going through.

The reason many of us don't go through is because the valley is too messy to get through. COVID-19 has been messy. People are dying. Nobody wants to experience the death of loved ones. But just imagine if the first responders refused to help because it is messy. Imagine if the doctors and nurses said that they couldn't help anyone because it is messy. Imagine if a parent said to a toddler that they couldn't change his diaper because it is too messy.

Life is messy. And it will always be messy until we go through it to the other side. We have to deal with some mess in life. We can't avoid it, because when we avoid the mess, then we avoid the solution. Divorce is messy. Bankruptcy is messy. Losing a job is messy. But when we are faced with these valleys, we have to go through them. There are lessons to be learned in every valley. Growth can happen as we walk in the valley. We must keep moving forward and walk through it. Keep moving. The way to is through. Get up! You've been depressed for too long. Get up! You've been down too long. Get up! This isn't your home. This isn't the church. This isn't Zion. This is not Jerusalem. Get up.

Keep moving through the valley.

CHAPTER NINETEEN

"Dig a well"

HAVE YOU EVER had a cavity and said, "I'm not going to the dentist because it's going to hurt." When you didn't go to get the tooth repaired did it get better on its own? Of course not. Have you ever had car trouble? A part needed to be replaced, but you didn't want to go through the pain of paying the bill, so you decided to pretend it was fine and hoped for the best. Did your tires grow new tires? Did the engine heal itself? Did the oil clean itself? Of course not. In order to get the desired solution you have to pay the price, and feel that pain.

The way to your next miracle, the way to your breakthrough, the way to your deliverance, the way to your healing, the way to coming out of your isolation, is *through*.

How do we do it? *"Who passing through the valley of Baca make it a well..."* *Baca* means a valley of weeping. Many of us have shed tears lately. Sometimes to go through the valley we have to shed some tears. There will be sorrow, but we have to keep moving. And while we are passing by, we can make it a well. Because if you dig deep enough, either you will find water, or water will fill where you dug. So, in the place of your weeping, *dig a well*. In the place you are hurting, *dig a well*. God tells us that we will find hidden springs that He has provided. He has intentionally, purposely and deliberately put hidden springs down in the desert.

How do we dig wells? When you start praising, you are digging a well. When you begin worshiping, you are digging a well. When you start thanking the Lord, you are digging a well. When you start praying, you're digging a well. When you turn your eyes upon Jesus and trust and obey Him, you're digging a well. You can praise through your tears. You can thank God even with a broken heart.

When you are dealing with loss, grief, sorrow, or pain, you can dig a well. Keep on digging through it because, when you dig, you will find the very resources you need to get through the desert. The very resources you need to get through the valley. Go after it. Be intentional. Pray. Praise. Trust. Obey.

But what happens if you are digging and nothing is changing? What if you can't find the hidden spring? Then the rain from above will come down. Whether underneath you or over you, God will make provision for you.

When we dig, it not only blesses us, it blesses others. When you dig a well and the water fills it, when you move on, the next person who comes along will be able to enjoy the water from the well that you dug in your wilderness. Somebody will be blessed because you went through the valley. Your experience can benefit others going through the same valley. Someone will find what they are looking for because you walked through it first. You are going to be the resource that God uses to provide for someone else. Because of your digging someone else will not have to cry as long, or dig as hard.

Verse 7 says, *"They go from strength to strength..."* When you go through the valley of weeping and you dig and trust God and leave wells behind for others, you go from strength to strength. You don't come out of the valley the same way you went into it. You will be mightier. You will be more anointed. You will be more powerful. You will have more faith. You will trust God more. Because you go from strength to strength. You were at one level of strength, but you rise to the next level.

Where before the valley you trusted in yourself, or the government, or your paycheck, or your intellect, after the valley you trust in God and find your strength in Him. The joy of the Lord is our strength. We get stronger because we go through. In order to get *to* this strength, we have to go *through* the valley. And as you are going, you will realize that nothing comes easy. Nothing is cheap. But God tells us that He will make provision along the way to get us through.

David and others finally made it to the house of the Lord. Verses 9 and 10 says, *"Behold, O God our shield, and look upon the face of thine anointed. For a day in thy courts is better than a thousand. I had rather be a doorkeeper in the house of my God, than to dwell in the tents of wickedness."* The Psalmist is saying that he just wants to get back to the house of the Lord and the fellowship that is there. I want to be where the feast of the Lord is. And if I get back there, I would rather be a doorkeeper than ever again be outside the church. I will put a mask on. I will enforce social distancing. I will use hand sanitizer. I will get out the *Lysol* wipes and wipe the doors and seats down. I will disinfect. I will mop. I will do everything I can. Just let me get back into the house.

I will be the janitor, the doorkeeper, the usher, if only I can be in the house of the Lord.

Verse 11 says, *"For the Lord God is a sun and shield: the Lord will give grace and glory: no good thing will he withhold from them that walk uprightly."* A shield is protection. But there are two times in scripture when *sun* is representative of restoration. Whatever you lost while going through, God will restore it. Just get back to church. God will restore and protect you.

Verse 12 says, *"O Lord of hosts, blessed is the man that trusteth in thee."* The Bible says we are all members one to another. We have all been fashioned for fellowship. The church is about community. The church is about living and breathing individuals. The church is never about solitary saints. The church is never about housebound saints forever, or housebound hermits. Isolation of the saints deprives the saints of fellowship.

In order for the church to be effective, there must be fellowship. In other words, there has to be more than one fellow in the ship. God has joined us together. We are joint heirs in Christ. He has fitted and gritted and knitted us together. He has helped us together.

And one day we shall be caught up together.

For a body to fulfill its purpose, every organ must be connected in its right place. Each part must function correctly so that the whole body can function. Only when all of the parts, gifts, and talents are in the right place can the body of Christ thrive. David knew he had to get to church because it was a place of blessing and healing and support. It was a place of encouragement and building up. It was a place where he could be free and have the liberty to praise and worship God in His manifest presence.

God has His name on the door, and if you go through the door, He will meet you there. Where two or more are gathered together in a Bible-based, God-fearing church, He is there. We need the church.

God is telling us that the way we will get back to church is to go through the valley. Today the valley is a pandemic, and all of the other troubles that happen as a result. But I know God is saying that we are getting closer to the end of the valley. And when you are going through it, start looking for the destination. The church.

Some people get comfortable in the valley. It is human nature to get comfortable with things that may not be good for us. God doesn't want anyone getting comfortable live streaming at home on a regular basis when the church is open. God wants us to not forsake the assembling together.

Some assembly is required.

CHAPTER TWENTY

"A letter of Assurance"

"For God is not unrighteous to forget your work and labour of love, which ye have shewed toward his name, in that ye have ministered to the saints, and do minister. And we desire that every one of you do shew the same diligence to the full assurance of hope unto the end: that ye be not slothful, but followers of them who through faith and patience inherit the promises. For when God made promise to Abraham, because he could swear by no greater, he sware by himself saying, Surely blessing I will bless thee, and multiplying I will multiply thee. And so,

after he had patiently endured, he obtained the promise. For men verily swear by the greater: and an oath for confirmation is to them an end of all strife. Wherein God, willing more abundantly to shew unto the heirs of promise the immutability of his counsel, confirmed it by an oath: that by two immutable things, in which it was impossible for God to lie, we might have a strong consolation, who have fled for refuge to lay hold upon the hope set before us: which hope we have as an anchor of the soul, both sure and stedfast, and which entereth into that within the veil; whither the forerunner is for us entered, even Jesus, made an high priest for ever after the order of Melchisedec." — Hebrews 6:10-20

THE BOOK OF Hebrews confounds many people. It's a little tricky, because we're not certain who wrote it. Some say it appears to be Paul, and some say it could even be Barnabas, while others suggest Apollos. But one thing we understand is that it was an *apostolic letter* or a *general letter*, which means it was a letter to the *whole* body of Christ.

The letter was written because the children of God were going through difficult times. Some of them were in danger of falling by the wayside. False doctrines had taken over, and a lot of them probably felt like God was not going to come through, so the "old ways" had become attractive to them. In chapter six, the writer lets us know that there is no other means of salvation.

> *"For it is impossible for those who were once enlightened, and have tasted of the heavenly gift, and were made partakers of the Holy Ghost, and have tasted the good word of God, and the powers of the world to come, if they shall fall away, to renew them again unto repentance; seeing they crucify to themselves the Son of God afresh, and put him to an open shame."*

In other words, there's no other baptism. There's no other sacrifice. Jesus is not coming back again to go through the pain and agony of Calvary to save us all over again. Basically, we have to grasp hold of what we already have. The word *assurance* means a positive declaration intended to give confidence. Some of the synonyms are *promise*, a *pledge*, a *guarantee*, a *vow*, an *oath*, a *word of honor*, a *commitment*, a *truth*, a *word*, a *bond*.

A letter of assurance.

The Bible lets us know in verse 18: *"...that by two immutable things, in which it was impossible for God to lie, we might have a strong consolation..."* That word *consolation* means moral support or encouragement. It means reassurance of the assurance, comfort to one who has suffered. It also means to mightily encourage.

God is writing a letter to the church to mightily encourage us, to assure us, and reassure us that whatever God starts, He finishes, and that in uncertain times, when you're going through difficult times, there's one thing you can bank on every time: the Word of God.

The writer starts by talking about how God made a promise to Abraham. God promised Abraham and Sarah that they would have a child. He would be a blessing. The father, Abram, turned into Abraham, the father of many nations. We know that for 24 years he was tempted and tested. Sometimes he was discouraged and he made a few foolish mistakes along the way.

But in the end, God's word was fulfilled.

Along the same line, God has a word for us. We cannot go by what we see or feel or how difficult things may look. God is saying, "I have given you an assurance, and that is my word." Verse 13: *"For when God made promise to Abraham, because he could swear by no greater, he sware by himself..."* God made a promise to Abraham. It's like when we go to court before a judge. We put our hand on the Bible and take an oath, "So help me God." God *is* God, so he couldn't swear to anyone, so he swore to himself that this would take place.

Verse 18 says: *"...that by two immutable things, in which it was impossible for God to lie, we might have a strong consolation, who have fled for refuge to lay hold upon the hope set before us..."*

God is saying, "I have a word for you Hebrew saints, the ones who are discouraged, the ones who are faint, the ones who are disoriented because of what they see and hear."

And God has a word for us today.

Pandemic. *Pan* means the whole of man. *Pandemic* comes from *pandemonium*, which, in some writings, refers to a place where demons dwell and run rampant. And *virus* comes from the Latin word *venom*. God is saying this venom that has infected the whole world, all of man, and caused pandemonium.

God is saying, "I've got a word for you. You cannot determine your future based on what you hear, based on what you see, and based on how impossible things may appear." God says, "I came to give you strong confidence and mightily encourage you that I'm still in control, and what I told you I would do in your life, I will do. There is nothing greater than me."

Now, the challenge we have today is believing God through his Word. One of the things I've learned about human nature is when things are going well, we don't have any problem trusting God, but when we're going through uncertainty and we're disoriented and the world has been turned upside down, it's much harder to trust God.

One of the keys to trusting God is *knowledge of the character of God*. What kept Job from turning against God and not cursing God out after he lost everything? He had a relationship with God. What kept Joseph faithful as he went from the pit to the prison and feeling like God had forsaken him? He had a relationship with God. What kept David when Saul was pursuing him? David had a relationship with God.

During these trying times, tap into your knowledge of and experience with God. Has he ever let you down before? Has he ever made a way out of no way? Has he ever removed a mountain nobody else could move? Has there ever been a day when you starved to death? Did he heal you when the doctors gave you a bad report? Did you get the raise when they didn't want to give you a raise? And if you *didn't* get the raise, did he still keep food on your table and clothing on your back?

You have to go back to the character of God, and you have to know him. God gave me an analogy. The IRS knows some things about us. The IRS knows where you work. They know how many kids you have. They know how much money you make. They know how much you spend on medical bills. They know your mortgage. They know your age. They know your status, if you're single, if you're married. But the average person at the IRS doesn't know you.

They wouldn't be able to recognize you from anybody else at the grocery store. They have some information on you, but they don't know you. Your pet knows you better, can recognize you better than someone at the IRS can, because they're familiar with your voice, your face, and your scent.

CHAPTER TWENTY-ONE

"One thing that does not change"

ANOTHER KEY TO trusting God is *knowledge of the Word of God*. In times of uncertainty, we must tap into the Word of God, and not only tap into it, but we must know it. In times of perplexity and confusion, with everything changing, there's one thing that does not change: that's God's Word. It is forever settled.

But here's the thing: I can't just know the Scripture. I have to know how to apply it to my life. Jesus even said, *"In this world you shall have trouble, tribulations, but be of good cheer, because I have overcome them."* It is the Word that's the same. It is the

Word that keeps us. It says: *"And so, after he had patiently endured, he obtained the promise. For men verily swear by the greater: and an oath for confirmation is to them an end of all strife. Wherein God, willing more abundantly to shew unto the heirs of promise the immutability of his counsel, confirmed it by an oath..."*

God is letting us know to be patient. I heard someone describe being patient *this* way: letting your motor idle when you feel like stripping the gears. I love that. When you feel like putting your foot to the pedal, but you do not do it. *"And so, after he had patiently endured..."* Endured. *"In your patience possess ye your souls."* That word—*endured*—literally means abiding under. I am under something, but I am enduring. It is not taking me down. In other words, I can handle this with the help of the Lord.

In the educational system, there's something called an *ABD*. It stands for All But Dissertation. It means I have taken all of the classes, I have passed all of the exams, I've even entered into candidacy for my PhD, but at some point, for a variety of reasons, I have not completed the dissertation. The dissertation being completed gives me that diploma—the paper proof that I'm now a master in this field. *ABD* means I'm almost there, but I'm not quite there. Most folks would not get to ABD.

God is saying if you patiently endure, when you come out of this, you're going to have some proof that you mastered this thing. "COVID-19 did not master me." *Endure*: actively abide under a trial with faith in God as your foundation. In other words, I can't endure just because I have a strong will. I can't endure just because I have a few extra bucks. The only way I'm going to endure *this* trial is with faith in God as my foundation.

That's the only way.

Verse 18: *"...that by two immutable things, in which it was impossible for God to lie, we might have a strong consolation, who have fled for refuge to lay hold upon the hope set before us..."* In Biblical times, there were six cities of refuge: three on the east side of Jordan and three on the west side of Jordan. If someone accidentally killed someone (manslaughter), if they were able to flee to those cities and get inside the gates, as long as they stayed there, nobody could harm them.

Jesus is *our* refuge. Before Jesus came, a high priest would intercede for the people, but now Jesus is our High Priest. What surprises us does not surprise him. Nothing can touch us without his approval. He is responsible for the care of those who belong to him, and here is his record: he has never, ever lost anyone.

The Lord is my refuge. He's my storm cellar when life sends a tornado. The Lord is my refuge. He is my fallout shelter when events explode all around me. The Lord is my refuge. He is my high tower when waves come crashing against me. God is my refuge, my strength, my hope, my trust, my safety net, and a very present help in the time of trouble.

That's the Lord we serve.

"...which hope we have as an anchor of the soul..." The Lord knew you and I would be where we are now, because he knows the world is *unstable*. He knew there would be times when the world would be uncertain. He knew there would be times when leaders would not know what to do, because the world is like a restless sea. Sometimes it's calm, but sometimes it's unstable, sometimes it's shaking, sometimes it's dangerous, sometimes it's unpredictable, and sometimes it's downright scary.

God knew that. He knew we're subject to change. He knew we're affected by contrary winds. We're like ships driven by winds, and we move wherever the wind moves us. That's our life. But understand, a ship is a vehicle designed to take us to our destiny. God is saying, "When the ship is rocking, when it looks like the ship is going to be capsized, I have an answer for that."

There are four different types of winds. There's an east wind, there's a west wind, there's a north wind, and there is a south wind. The Bible mentions all four. When the Bible mentions the north wind, it's usually related to construction or constructing. When the Bible mentions the south wind, it's usually related to a gentle, warm, blowing wind. The Bible mentions the west wind one time in Exodus 10:19. That's when God used a west wind to blow away the locusts that were a plague in Egypt into the Red Sea.

And then there is the east wind. The east wind is mentioned 19 times in the Bible, twice as much as all of the other winds together. Whenever the Bible mentions the east wind, it's always the cause of destruction, ruin, havoc, or chastisement. The Bible says when it came to Pharaoh's dream with Joseph, seven ears of corn were blasted by the east wind. Job 27:21 says, *"The east wind carrieth him away, and he departeth: and as a storm…"* Remember Jonah when he was under the gourd at Nineveh?

It was an east wind that took away Jonah's shade.

Ezekiel says the east wind dries up fruit and withers the crops. It is the east wind that destroys. Well, in 2020, an east wind came into the world. COVID-19 did not come from the west, did not come from the north, did not come from the south. As big as China is, it came from a city called Wuhan that is in the east central part of China. So, an eastern city within an eastern nation was the source of an east wind that blew across the world and affected everybody.

When the east wind comes, there's always destruction. There are a few times when God allowed the east wind to come to chastise his children. The east wind scatters. The east wind destroys. The east wind chastises. But God is saying, "When the east wind comes, you have an anchor."

An anchor's job is to keep the crew and the passengers safe. An anchor enables the ship to stay on its course and reach its destination. An anchor looks for something solid below that it can latch onto. An anchor goes down and grabs on something below that you *can't* see so you can deal with what's above that you *can* see. God has an anchor for every believer. We can ride this out.

We *will* ride this out.

That's how I know we will come out of this. We will make it because God has given us a letter of assurance. "I don't want you to be tossed to and fro. I don't want you feeling helpless and hopeless. I don't want you scared and terrified. I have given you an anchor to hold you in the midst of the storm. In the midst of the contrary east wind that's blowing that's trying to capsize your boat, there is an anchor."

An anchor is a device usually made out of iron that connects the vessel to the bed or the body of water to prevent it from drifting, wrecking, crashing, or capsizing. There are what they call *hooking anchors*, and they hold the ship together by hooking onto something on the seabed, such as a rock.

There are *sheer mass anchors*. Those are the ones that are so heavy that even if the boat is out in the middle of the water and it can't go down in the water, the weight of it is so heavy the boat doesn't drift.

Then there are *sea anchors*. They act like braces. When the waves are pounding, they keep it on a course.

God wants us to know there will not be a *Titanic* disaster with the body of Christ. We started 2020 not knowing we needed an anchor. We were too busy looking at our visions, counting our money, and going after our dreams, but God saw an east wind coming. A strong wind from Wuhan, China.

And it has turned the world upside down.

CHAPTER TWENTY-TWO

"We have an anchor"

WHEN THE TRIALS of life come, when it seems like things are exploding around you, when leaders don't have an answer, when the physicians don't have an answer, when the authorities don't have an answer, God is saying, "I have made preparation for the saints of God," so that we will not experience shipwreck in the midst of the storm. We have an anchor that is strong, secure, and steady. No storm, no typhoon, no hurricane, and no tempest can overwhelm the anchor, because the anchor is Jesus.

Let the winds blow. Let the storm come. I shall not be capsized or terrorized because I have an anchor. An anchor is used to bring comfort, especially in the midst of the storm. God is saying, "I've given you some assurance. I've given you an anchor. You don't have to be disoriented. You don't have to be confused. You don't have to give up. You don't have to lose your way." An anchor provides peace. An anchor provides assurance. An anchor provides blessed assurance and comfort that everything is going to be all right.

You and I have an anchor today, and the strength of the anchor is based on the word of the one who made the promise. The Bible says it was God who made the promise. It was God who made the oath. It was God himself who said, "You have an anchor," in order to give peace and hope, so we don't give up in uncertain times. The anchor has the capacity to hold us when the wind is blowing. In times of uncertainty, darkness, and peril, God has given us an anchor.

An anchor is meant to be dropped to the depths. It lodges among the rocks, and it holds the ship in a steady position throughout the storm. The boat may rock a little bit, and you may have to be patient for a while, because it may even stop making progress. What we have to understand, as saints, is not only does God order our steps, sometimes God orders our *stops*.

And God has stopped the world.

Let me say it again. The same God who orders our steps also orders our stops. You may hear the wind howling. You may hear the ship creaking and the mast flapping, but your anchor will hold. It is sure. It cannot slip. It is steadfast, which means it cannot break. Why? Because an anchor is something that's outside of the ship helping those *inside* the ship. *Our* anchor is something outside of us helping us deal with what's going on. The Holy Ghost is inside of us, but Jesus, our High Priest, is interceding for us to help us so that we do not drown.

An anchor gives you rest. *"Come unto me, all ye that labour and are heavy laden, and I will give you rest."* God is saying to the saints of God, "I want you to rest." "But, Pastor, you don't know what's going on." God says, "Rest." God says, "Don't get discouraged. Don't give up." God says, "Rest," because you and I have an anchor. Job 34:29 says, *"When he giveth quietness, who then can make trouble?"* When God quiets your spirit, when God says, "Peace, be still," who can make trouble?

In the midst of trouble, God is saying, "Peace, be still." It keeps the ship from losing ground. You haven't lost any ground. As a matter of fact, when we come out of this, I'm praying that we'll come out of this with greater faith, greater anointing, greater trust. It is God who is our anchor. It doesn't do any good having an anchor unless you have something solid to hold it.

My hope is built on nothing less
Than Jesus' blood and righteousness;
I dare not trust the sweetest frame
But wholly trust in Jesus' name.

When darkness seems to hide his lovely face,
I'll rest on his unchanging grace;
In every high and stormy gale,
My anchor holds within the veil.

On Christ the solid rock I stand,
All other ground is sinking sand,
All other ground is sinking sand.

Understand this: the larger the vessel, the stronger the cable chains must be to hold the anchor. There's the anchor, but there also must be the cable chains. Your chain must be connected to the anchor so that when the storm comes, it does not pull the ship away. Jesus is our anchor, and He's the one who holds us. He's the one who's keeping us right now.

As we go through what's going on right now, there's an anchor that's holding us. It's good that a ship has a hold upon the anchor, but it's more important that the anchor keeps its hold on the ship. We are the ship. The anchor is Jesus, and the anchor is holding up the ship. That's why you have not capsized: because better than the ship having the anchor is the anchor having hold of the ship.

God is saying, "Because I'm the anchor and I have ahold of the ship and I've given you an oath and a promise and I can't lie, you have an assurance and a reassurance that you're coming out of this on the other side."

When the Devil whispers in your ear that you're about ready to capsize, have you heard a voice saying, "I've got you"? When the Devil tries to make you panic, have you heard a voice saying, "I won't let you go"? When the Devil is saying, "I just don't know how we're going to get out," have you heard a voice saying, "I'll never leave you. I'll never forsake you. Yea, though you walk through the valley of the shadow of death, you don't have to fear any evil, because I'm with you"?

Even if you've been infected, and even for those saints of God who have taken their last breath due to COVID-19, God is saying, "You'll never have to go through this alone. We're going to go through this together, and if I have to usher you to the other side of eternity, I'll do that. But know this: you are safe with me. I didn't save you for a moment; I saved you for eternity." So, you have an anchor, and that anchor is Jesus. It is safe. It is secure.

I am anchored in Jesus. My soul is anchored in Jesus. My hopes are anchored in Jesus. My future is anchored in Jesus. My dreams are anchored in Jesus. My eternal destination is anchored in Jesus. I say to every believer: stay anchored. Why is it so important? Because when man runs out of ideas, when man runs out of options, when man runs out of ventilators and test kits and masks and the problem is still there, man needs something bigger than man.

The story is told about some passengers who were on a ship. The ship ran into a storm. The captain was very seasoned. One of the passengers came up to him and said, "We're in great danger, aren't we?" At first, the captain looked like he didn't even see him. The ship was rocking, going back and forth. So, the person shouted a little louder and said, "Hey, Captain, we're in great danger, aren't we?"

The captain looked at the person and said, "Yes." The person asked, "Should we be afraid?" The captain said, "Yes. There is plenty to fear but not one thing to feel like you're in danger of." He said, "Not one bit of danger. The ship is rocking. It's going to make you nervous. It's going to unsettle you for a while, but you aren't in any danger, because this captain has weathered storms, and I know how to get you to your destination. So, fear, but no danger. You're going to get to the other side."

There was a great missionary to China in the 19th century named Hudson Taylor. He was on a ship and in waters where there was no wind. It was just drifting to a shore. The problem was the shore it was drifting to was inhabited by cannibals, and if the ship landed there, the cannibals were going to have a nice feast that night. One of the captains came down to Hudson Taylor's stateroom and said, "You're a praying man, right?"

He said, "Yes."

"Will you please pray to the Lord to help us? We need some winds to come to help get us on course so we don't drift to this island full of cannibals."

Hudson Taylor told him to set up the sails to catch the breeze.

The captain said, "I'm not going to look like a fool. There's no breeze out here, and I'm not going to be the laughingstock of my men. If a wind comes, I'll set up the sail, but I'm not going to set it up now. There's no breeze."

Hudson Taylor told him, "Well, I won't pray until you set the sails." So, the captain, after huffing and puffing, got his men to set the sails, to prepare the sails. While Hudson Taylor was down in the stateroom praying, there was a knock on the door. It was the captain, who asked him, "Are you still praying for wind?"

"Yes," Taylor said.

"Well, would you please stop? Right now, we have more wind than we can handle."

We must pray for God to send a west wind. The east wind brought the locusts, the plague, to Egypt. And it brought COVID-19. The only thing that can get rid of the effects of an east wind is a west wind. God sent the west wind to push the locusts that came from the east wind into the Red Sea. We have to pray God sends a west wind to get rid of all the death and destruction and the effects that have been caused by the east wind.

God is saying, "While you are praying for the west wind, stay anchored in me. You have an assurance, a letter from me that you're going to come out of this okay."

Our prayer must be, "Oh Lord, send a west wind!"

CHAPTER TWENTY-THREE

"Your best won't pass the test"

THERE'S A DOCUMENTARY that has been on that has been amazing and very entertaining in a time when it's hard to find some good entertainment. It is called *The Last Dance*, and it's about Michael Jordan's last year with the Chicago Bulls. Both Jordan and his coach, Phil Jackson, allowed a film crew to shadow them that year. They came up with a 10-part documentary that planned for release summer of 2020, but since all of us are bored and wanted something to watch during the pandemic they moved it up. I think it was an act of mercy. Though the documentary includes Jackson, it is centered around Jordan, who is considered the GOAT—Greatest Of All Time. He was hesitant to do it, actually waiting 10 years, saying, "I don't want people to get the wrong idea and look at me differently than they have all of these years because of my intensity and my competitiveness."

I grew up a Bulls fan, so I agree that he's the greatest of all time. And in the documentary, you find out that winning was number one with Michael. Everything else took second place. Everything. Michael wanted to do nothing but win, and to win at all costs. So, when you see the documentary, you see a lot of the flaws of the great one. He has been called a bully. He has been called selfish. He has been called a whole lot of different names.

In the final episode, he even broke down and started crying when he said that people didn't understand that he never forced anybody else to do anything he would not do and it was all about winning. He stopped the cameras. But in that, we have a chance to see Michael in a way we had never seen him before. What is interesting is that not only do we still see his greatness (a lot of young people said, "Now I understand why he's considered the greatest of all time"), but we're also seeing Michael's flaws.

It is so interesting, because when you look at the Word of God, one of the things God does is that He never attempts to portray the men and women He used as plastic saints with shiny halos. The Bible lets us know that God uses people, but we see that the people God uses are not perfect. Far from it. They have flaws. God has set it up so there is no hero worshiping in the Bible. Noah built an ark, saved the world, but Noah got drunk one night. Jacob was one of the biggest liars and schemers. Even today, he could outwit most folks. Moses had a bad temper, so bad he missed the Promised Land.

Do you remember Elijah? Suicidal, under a juniper tree. "I'm not better than the others. Lord, just take my life." Peter, who told the Lord, "If everybody denies you, don't worry about Pete. Pete has got your back. I've got you." But when someone asked, "Weren't you with Jesus?" he denied it and then finally cussed them out. "Leave me alone. Get out of here." Jonah went one direction when God told him to go another direction.

No perfect people.

In the Bible, every character is fully human. They are real people. One of the reasons God has put fully human, real people in the Bible is so you and I will have no trouble identifying with some of them when we go through our situations. In the Bible, there are no perfect husbands. In the Bible, there are no perfect wives. In the Bible, there are no perfect sons. There are no perfect daughters. There are no perfect prophets and no perfect kings. In the Bible, we all have flaws. But as we delve into the Word of God, we see that it helps us when we get into imperfect situations.

And David said in his heart, I shall now perish one day by the hand of Saul: there is nothing better for me than that I should speedily escape into the land of the Philistines; and Saul shall despair of me, to seek me any more in any coast of Israel: so shall I escape out of his hand." David said, "I have a really good plan." "And David arose, and he passed over with the six hundred men that were with him unto Achish, the son of Maoch, king of Gath." – I Samuel 27:1-2

David had been anointed as King by Samuel, but he is ignored by most people. There's a lesson right there. The world can overlook you, pass you by, think that you have nothing you can offer, but God has a way of looking at the overlooked. As a matter of fact, many times God will hide you so that you *are* overlooked until your time comes.

So, David was anointed king. Now, you would think that it's something that would happen quickly and David would soon be on the throne. No, no, no. It is somewhere between 15 to 20 years before David sat on the throne in Zion. Whenever God anoints you, get ready for hell, because with every title comes a test, with every office comes some obstacles, and with every position comes peril.

In I Samuel chapter 16, David is anointed. In chapter 17, there's a big giant by the name of Goliath. Everybody is afraid of him, but David takes him out. In chapter 18, Saul is upset because the folks are singing, "Saul killed a thousand…" which in most cases would be a compliment. "…but David killed his ten thousand." Saul becomes jealous, envious, and an evil spirit came over Saul.

One of the things we're dealing with in *this* day and age is not just COVID-19, but evil on a level we have not seen in our lives. There are evil spirits trying to do everything they can to destroy us, destroy our nation, destroy our cities, destroy our families, destroy our churches, destroy our ministries, destroy our marriages, destroy our children.

Evil is on the rampage.

Saul had an evil spirit, and the Bible says he picked up a javelin and tried to nail David against the wall with it. When Saul did not kill him, he acted like he just made a mistake, a little crazy. But clearly, by this time Saul was paranoid and wanted nothing to do with David. David hung in there as long as he could, but after a while, anyone would get tired of dodging javelins.

A sword is meant for close combat. Even a spear is meant for somewhat close combat, but javelins are meant for distance. Somebody can throw a javelin at you, and you may not even see it. A sword you may see, a spear you may see, but javelins are big. They're heavy. They're sharp. A whole lot of saints have gone down because somebody pinned them to the wall with a javelin they didn't see coming—javelins of jealousy, javelins of bitterness, javelins of hate.

At some point, David got tired of dodging javelins and by the time we get to chapter 24, David was in a cave with a group of malcontents. They were ex-criminals, who didn't have much to offer, but God sent them to David. One of the lessons for David to learn was about compassion. God will send folks into your life who don't have what you have, so that you can learn how to be compassionate toward those who are in a worse situations. In chapter 25, David met Abigail and her foolish husband, Nabal.

In chapter 26, David seemed to be at a spiritual high. One of his men wanted to take out Saul while Saul was in the cave relieving himself. David took his spear and his water container, but he did not touch Saul. On three occasions he had an opportunity to take out Saul, but he would not do it. David said, "I will not touch the Lord's anointed." As a matter of fact, last time he told Abner, "You should be fired from your position, because you didn't cover the king."

The king was trying to kill David, but David rebuked his armor-bearer. At this point, David was certain that he's in the hands of God. David is anointed. But then something happened between chapter 26 and chapter 27. It seems to suggest a close proximity between the two, because it doesn't seem like there was a big gap. There was no crisis here that would have prompted David to do what he did. As a matter of fact, in chapter 26, verse 10, David told them, "I don't have to kill Saul because the Lord will take him out." David said that God will kill him. God will take him out.

But here, David is saying, "Saul will kill me." David is saying, "I'm going to die." The same David who said, "Don't you touch the anointed." David was so confident in God. David was a pillar of faith, but something happens between chapter 26 and 27. David decides, "I'm getting ready to die if I don't flee." So, David begins to think, "The only safe place for me is a place where Saul won't look for me or is dangerous if he comes, so I'm going to go to the land of the Philistines."

Why is David going to the land of the Philistines? Is he tired? Probably. Is he impatient? Probably. Is David full of doubt and unbelief? Probably. But it has been eight long years, and David has been running from Saul. David has been a fugitive. It has been eight long years, and eight long years of any test will start wearing you down at some point.

I don't care how anointed you are.

Eight years of day-to-day watching your back. Can you imagine that? Eight years of week-to-week watching your back. Eight years, hour by hour, month to month, watching your back, never really feeling like you can rest because you know someone is after you. David is in a tight spot. David is feeling the pressure. He's feeling that Saul is closing in on him.

CHAPTER TWENTY-FOUR

"Stinking thinking"

DAVID SAID, "THE only thing I can do to save myself is to go and dwell with the Philistines." Remember, this is David who, many times, in the Psalms would write about what he was going through. "Where was God? Why don't you do something? O Lord, why do you stand so far away from me? How long will you forget me, Lord? Will it be forever? How long do I have to put up with this? My enemies are all around me."

Do these words sound familiar to some of you? "How long, God? Where are you, God? Why don't you do something? I'm in a tight place. I'm in a tight jam. I'm in a tight situation, God, and it seems like you won't do anything. It looks like you've left me to take care of myself. It looks like you've left me to decide what is best for me." There's no pat answer. We don't know. But there's a truth you have to grab ahold of: *God has not deserted you.* God has a plan for you.

David said, "The best I can do under the situation, since God seems to not be in the picture anymore, is to go into the land of the Philistines." David thought to himself. That's what we call *stinkin' thinkin'.* He starts thinking. He starts weighing his options. I'm talking to some folks right now. You're weighing your options in a tight situation. You're weighing your options in a tight jam. You're weighing your options because you're shut in.

During the pandemic I've listened to the media talk about our leaders trying to weigh their options. "When will we open? How much can open? What states can open? Will we get a vaccine? How many will we test? When can we test them?" They're trying to weigh all of their options based on man's intelligence.

David is doing that. David is now rationalizing. David is now becoming logical. David has lost his identity. David has lost his purpose. David is now disillusioned. One of the great definitions of discouragement is when reality meets expectation and the expectations are negative. We tend to become discouraged.

Here is David now. David says, "The best I can do is go to the land of the Philistines." This is David, the man who killed a bear at a young age, killed a lion at a young age, killed Goliath when nobody else was willing to take him on. But right now, David is literally having a faith breakdown.

David was a man who would usually inquire. He would always go before God for direction, for guidance. He would sit before God. "God, what should I do? What should I do?" But there is no indication of David praying. There's no indication of David fasting. There's no indication of David seeking wise counsel. What David didn't realize is if he had just gone before God...

Nobody can hide you like Jesus. Go ask Brother Moses, "Can the Lord hide you?" For 40 years he hid him in the desert. Go ask the two spies, "Can God hide you?" Yes. Even if he has to put you in the house of a prostitute, God can hide you. "Brother Elijah, can he hide you?" Yes, he can, and he will send your meals by delivery by a raven. Can he hide you? Even Jesus, Mary and Joseph had to take him to Egypt to hide.

God is the master of social distancing.

So, the Holy Ghost is saying, "David, you should not have ever put a period where God has put a comma." David thought Saul would never look for him in the land of the Philistines.

But, David, look at yourself. Think about what you're doing. The Philistines aren't your friends. The Philistines aren't the ones who love you. The Philistines probably hate you even more than Saul does because you killed their champion. David, what are you thinking? His nerves have gone. David has had a breakdown.

You will never, ever escape your enemy by running back into his camp.

The world will tell you, "Oh yeah. The saints aren't treating you right. The saints are mistreating you. The pastor is mistreating you. Serving the Lord has not paid off. It seems like you had a better life before." The world will tell you, "You need to come back out here." Satan is always trying to get God's children to come back out into the world, but what you have to understand is that you cannot go forward by going backward. You cannot go up by going down. You cannot make progress by going around in circles.

David thinks, "I can go rest in the land of my enemy, and somehow or another, I'm going to get to Zion." No. You cannot progress to Zion by resting in the land of your enemy. What's happening now is that David has thought about it. David has pondered it. David has meditated. David tried to rationalize and tried to figure out what he must do, but understand, when you're in a tight jam, a tight fix, you need to *wait* for God. Being called by God will never be easy. You will never have an easy life when the anointing of God is on you, and the greater the anointing, the greater the test. Many times, we don't understand the anointing God has put on us.

God is saying, "I have a destiny for you. I have a calling, but it will not be easy. You've been saved too long to go back. You've been delivered too long to go back. David, you've cried too many tears. You've had too many sleepless nights. There was too much fasting and praying and shut-ins and midnight prayer."

How did David end up in the land of the Philistines, thinking that his best was good enough? David weighed his options *without God*. David rationalized his decisions without God. David strategized without God. The biggest enemy was not Saul; the biggest enemy was David's own mind. It was David's mind that was giving the best to him.

There is a saying, "When you're in your own mind, you're behind enemy lines."

"David, your thinking is out of control. Your thinking is not in line with the Word of God. Your thinking is not where it should be. David, you know what God can do." But sometimes we become so smart we forget about God. Understand, your best is not good enough with your PhD self. Your best is not good enough with your MBA self. Your best is not good enough with your post-doctorate self. Your best is not good enough with your BS and your BA self.

Your best will never pass life's test.

There are some things in life that will kill us if we don't go through them with God. Your best won't pass the test. Saul is going to kill you. "David, you're good at hiding in trouble, but you have to understand that it was not you in the first place. I know folks are saying, 'Saul killed a thousand and David killed ten thousand,' but, David, it wasn't you. It must have gotten to your head. You must have thought it was you. David, you're not thinking rationally. You're not thinking logically. You're not thinking spiritually. David, do you really think you were supposed to kill Goliath? Do you really think you are quick enough to dodge javelins that are being thrown at you? Do you really think that?"

God is saying, "You weren't supposed to kill the bear. You weren't supposed to beat the lion. You weren't supposed to beat Goliath. But, David, something happened. I covered you."

You weren't supposed to beat cancer. You weren't supposed to beat COVID-19. You weren't supposed to beat that blood clot. You weren't supposed to beat that heart attack. You weren't supposed to beat diabetes. You weren't supposed to beat unemployment. You weren't supposed to beat that childhood. You weren't supposed to beat that abuse. You weren't supposed to beat that divorce. You weren't supposed to beat crazy. You weren't supposed to beat the teasing you got in school. You weren't supposed to beat low self-esteem. You weren't supposed to beat bankruptcy. You weren't supposed to beat the church split. You weren't supposed to beat the car accident. You weren't supposed to beat the mistake. You weren't supposed to beat the sickness. You weren't supposed to beat the failure. You weren't supposed to beat your bad temper. You weren't supposed to beat your smart mouth. You weren't supposed to beat your rebellious attitude. You weren't supposed to beat the evil spirit. You weren't supposed to beat alcohol. You weren't supposed to beat cocaine. You weren't supposed to beat marijuana. You weren't supposed to beat heroin. You weren't supposed to beat rejection and abandonment and hurt and pain.

But God is saying, "It was not you. You were covered."

"David, I covered you. You are alive not because your mind has taken you to the Philistines. David, it was me who would not let you die. It was me who would not allow you to fail. It was me who would not allow you to be defeated. It was me who would not allow you to lose your mind. It was me who wouldn't let you go crazy. It was me who wouldn't let you have a nervous breakdown. It was me who wouldn't allow you to get out there so far until my hands of grace and my hands of mercy could not pull you back. David, it was me who covered you. It was me who watched over you. It was never you; it was me. David, your best will never pass the test. Your best will not defeat Goliath. Your best will not kill a bear. Your best will not kill a lion. Your best will not kill Saul. Your best thinking will not stop death from coming after you and overtaking you."

"David, it was me."

CHAPTER TWENTY-FIVE

"How do we change stinking thinking"

YOUR BEST WILL never pass the test. If God doesn't move, all of us will perish. It takes God's wisdom. It takes God's knowledge. It takes God's power to help us overcome enemies trying to kill and destroy us. How do we change our thinking?

1. DON'T FALL INTO THE LONE RANGER SYNDROME.

We have this false sense of "aloneness." When you're going through a spiritual struggle, when you're dealing with pain, when you're dealing with crazy, when you're dealing with suffering, when you're about ready to have a faith breakdown or a nervous breakdown, don't be a Lone Ranger. Some of us think, "I can make it by myself. I can ride this out by myself." That frame of mind is dangerous, because you need me and I need you. Do not be a Lone Ranger.

2. BASE YOUR DECISIONS ON FAITH, NOT SIGHT.

Don't base your decisions on what you're seeing. David saw Saul coming at him, and all he could do was run, because he was certain he was going to die, and his only hope was in trying to, somehow or another, do something to save himself. That's not faith; that's fear. We don't move by sight. We walk by faith. You have to understand that.

3. DON'T FORGET WHAT YOU MUST REMEMBER.

David, how can Saul destroy you? The anointing was poured over your head from a ram's horn. God passed everybody else and anointed you. The Spirit of the Lord came down upon you. David, you know you can't be king until Saul is dead, but not that you have to kill Saul. Don't accept a lie as truth. You cannot be king until Saul is dead, so why are you entertaining these thoughts? Why are you being so foolish, when God told you that you have to get to Zion, when God said you *will* go to Zion, when God said you *will* be king?

God is saying, "David, don't forget what you need to remember." David, God saved you time and time and time again. Don't forget. God provided for you time and time and time again. Don't forget. Don't forget what you need to remember. I have to remember that all things work together for my good. I have to remember that there's no weapon formed against me that shall prosper. I have to remember that greater is He who is in me than he who is in the world. I have to remember that if I call on Jesus, He will answer prayer. I have to remember that He may not come when I want him to come, but He's always right on time. I have to remember He knows my name. He knows where I stay. He knows my frame. He knows my thoughts. I have to remember that He's the almighty, all-powerful, all-seeing, ever-present, uncreated, unchangeable God. I have to remember that.

Don't forget what you need to remember.

"It was not Saul who told you you're going to be king; it was me. David, I don't care how many javelins are thrown at you. I don't care how many swords come at you. I don't care how many giants try to take you down. I don't care how many evil kings come at you. If I said it, it will not return unto me void. David, you shall be king, but in a time of being in a tight spot, a tight squeeze, a tight jam, you started thinking too much. You started massaging your thoughts. You started rationalizing too much, and you lost your way. David, you have to get yourself together."

4. WHEN I'M TRYING TO THINK FOR MYSELF IN A BAD SITUATION, MANY TIMES, THE BEST THING I CAN DO IS REST.

Rest in the Lord and realize that your best won't pass the test. David killed a bear. David killed a lion. I hear the Lord saying, "David, it wasn't your best killing the lion and killing the bear or killing Goliath that qualified you. Doing your best made you a candidate for destiny, but it was not your best that qualified you. When your best ended, when your capabilities ended, *then* perfection started."

What does God do? God takes our best, and then he breathes on it. God takes our best, and then he touches it. God takes our best, and then he anoints it. So, David, quit telling me that you're doing your best and nothing has changed. You're just at the end of your limitations. You're just at the end of your knowledge. You're just at the end of your wisdom. You're just at the end of your hookups. You're just at the end of your ideas. You're just at the end of your plans. You're just at the end of your thoughts, at the end of your scheming, at the end of your dealings. You're just at the end of trying to work it out yourself.

I hear the songwriter saying, "Jesus can work it out." When Jacob tried to do his best, he ran into trouble with Esau. When Moses tried to do his best, he ended up being a fugitive. When David tried to do his best, he ended up living with the Philistines, the enemies of Israel. God is saying, "When you come to the end of your best, only then will the process of perfection start. Don't get weary. Don't get tired. Don't give up. Oh yeah, that's a price tag on your head. Oh yeah, Saul is trying to kill you, but your greatest enemy is your mind. It's not Saul that's killing you. It's not the Philistines, David; it is your mind that now has ahold of you, and you're having a faith breakdown, and you're trying to struggle to figure out how you can fix it yourself."

You can't fix COVID-19. You can't make a vaccine. You can't end the shut-in for a whole nation. Your best will not pass the test. God is saying, "David, if you trust me, if you depend on me, if you let me do it, I can work out what you can't work out." What are you thinking about doing right now without God? What strategies and plans have you put together right now without God? What is your mind telling you to do right now without God?

When you've done your best and nothing has changed, when you've done your best and the situation is still the same, it just means you're at the end of your capability. It means that God is saying to you, "I've been trying to get you alone by myself for a long time. Now that I've got you, watch me. I know your money is tight, but watch me stretch it. I know he or she dumped you, but watch me comfort you. I know what the doctor said, and it looks bleak, but watch me heal you. I know your kids are acting crazy, like they're the Devil's kids, acting like they never knew me, but get back. Wipe your tears. Watch me save them. Watch me deliver them. You will not find happiness in the camp of the Philistines. Your happiness is based on resting in me and then moving toward Israel. Find your rest in me, and then keep moving toward your goal, toward your destiny, toward your purpose. As you go forth and fight bigger giants and bigger enemies, just always remember, your best will never pass the test."

He who is struck by the lightning doesn't hear the thunder.

HUNGARIAN PROVERB

CHAPTER TWENTY-SIX

"Coming undone"

"Then the disciples went away again unto their own home. But Mary stood without at the sepulchre weeping: and as she wept, she stooped down, and looked into the sepulchre, and seeth two angels in white sitting, the one at the head, and the other at the feet, where the body of Jesus had lain. And they say unto her, Woman, why weepest thou?

She saith unto them, Because they have taken away my Lord, and I know not where they have laid him. And when she had thus said, she turned herself back, and saw Jesus standing, and knew not that it was Jesus. Jesus saith unto her, Woman, why weepest thou? whom seekest thou?

She, supposing him to be the gardener, saith unto him, Sir, if thou have borne him hence, tell me where thou hast laid him, and I will take him away. Jesus saith unto her, Mary. She turned herself, and saith unto him, Rabboni; which is to say, Master. Jesus saith unto her, Touch me not; for I am not yet ascended to my Father: but go to my brethren, and say unto them, I ascend unto my Father, and your Father; and to my God, and your God." – John 20:10-17

IN THIS PARTICULAR text, the two Mary's (although John only records one Mary, the other writers let us know it was two, Magdalene and Mary) have gone to the tomb. They're on their way to the tomb to dress the body of Jesus, to anoint the body of Jesus with the burial perfumes, because Jesus now is dead. The one they loved is dead.

It's interesting, because these are people who had seen their closest friend murdered, crucified, in one of the most vicious ways someone could die. They watched Him as he took His last breath and how He had cried out, and they stayed to the bitter end. In this day and time, it would be the equivalent of a lynching. They watched Him as He was stabbed in the side and died a slow and painful death.

They had hoped He would be the one who would free them from the Roman oppression and usher in a new age, but now *this* Jesus is dead. *Dead*, a word which means no longer living. It means without life, lacking warmth or interest or brightness, without feeling or motion or power. Dead.

So, they're on their way with the special spices. You must understand that they had waited until Sunday. Because of the Sabbath they had to wait. I imagine that wait probably seemed like days, probably weeks. When that Easter Sunday arrived, I imagine the two Marys could not wait to go and find the body of Jesus. Not only were they carrying with them their burial spices, but they were carrying despondency. They were carrying discouragement. They were carrying bewilderment. They were carrying fear. They were carrying hopelessness and helplessness.

There was only one task that remained, and that was to take care of His body. I imagine the grief was almost unbearable, because the one in whom they had placed their hope was dead. The one who had healed the sick and gave sight to the blind was dead. The one who said He was the Christ, the Messiah, was dead.

When you look at what was going on in their world, it's quite like what's going on in our world right now. Their world was coming apart, and Mary was coming undone. That's a word we don't hear a lot: *coming undone* or *coming apart*. So, I did a little research to see what this *coming undone* means.

One of the definitions is when we are unable to find relief, when we're unable to find peace. We come undone in the times of our greatest loss, our greatest failures. We come undone in times of uncertainty and unknowing, when you feel like your life is out of control. Many times, in old days, they said, "I have become undone." It means "My life is in ruin."

Undone means to untie, unwrap, unfasten. It also means to lose your composure and your self-control. When your world is coming undone, folks can't help you too much. Counselors are not a great help to you. Money won't fix it, because you're becoming undone. Things won't fix it, because you're becoming undone.

Things we're familiar with that used to help us in the past… Alcohol…Johnnie Walker Red or Black or even Blue will not fix it. Drugs will not fix it. Heroin will not fix it. Cocaine will not fix it. Marijuana will not fix it. Sex will not fix it. None of the familiar things that used to work to give us peace help us now, because we are coming undone. It means we have nowhere to turn and there's no letup.

This is what's going on right now in the world. The world has become undone.

COVID-19 has turned this world upside down, and we cannot see the future. In many cases, we can't reach back to the past and grab ahold of something that will help us at this time. The world is at a complete loss. People are exhausted. Leaders are exhausted. Physicians are exhausted. Spiritual leaders are exhausted. Politicians are exhausted. They're exhausted physically, mentally, and spiritually.

They've become undone.

When you become undone, it's hard to focus on those things on which you used to focus. Sometimes it's even hard to focus on the Lord. Sometimes it's hard to focus on prayer. Sometimes it's hard to focus on your devotional. The book of Psalms that helped so much is not helping that much right now because I am undone. I'm at a complete loss. Everything is out of focus.

Nothing is the same anymore.

The good news is that *undone* isn't a place God wants us to dwell. That's what the Devil wants. He wants you to believe that things will never change, that you'll always be undone. He wants you to believe this is the new normal: masks and social distancing. He wants you to believe you will never, ever find happiness again; you'll never, ever find peace again; you'll never, ever find joy again; you'll never be able to go back to your job with your coworkers, go back to the church with the saints. You will never be able to go back to school to get your degree with your friends, that everything will always be the way it is now.

I heard someone say that life is not tidy. We live in a world where there are a lot of questions with no answers. What's going on right now with COVID is that there's a tug-of-war between trust and joy, dread and fear. The world is full of unanswered questions, and we've been bringing them to the authorities, but the authorities are just as messed up as everyone else is, because they don't understand what's going on. So, we are uncomfortable, we are anxious, we are disturbed, because our world has been turned upside down and we're coming apart.

Mary's world was just like ours. It was coming apart. It was turned upside down, but she kept walking toward the tomb. I believe that's a word for everybody today. Regardless of how your world is turned upside down, coming apart, just start moving toward the tomb. She had shattered dreams. She was hurt, dealing with pain and heartache, but she kept walking toward the tomb. She kept pressing. She felt disillusioned, like many folks. She felt uncertain. She didn't have all of the answers and she had a whole lot of questions, but she kept walking toward the tomb. Her grief was almost unbearable, but she kept walking toward the tomb.

God is saying, we have to continue to walk toward the tomb. Perhaps Mary was seeking closure. Mary, no doubt, thought that the Lord was dead. Perhaps she was seeking closure, and somehow or another she felt that "This will help me to go on with life."

But something shocking happened. It blew their minds. They did not expect it. First of all, the stone was rolled away. Have you ever thought how these two women believed they were going to remove the stone? Do you think they even thought about that as they were moving toward the tomb? But, anyway, the stone has been removed, and the body is not there. The linen clothes are lying all around.

But no body.

So, Mary starts running. *"...and cometh to Simon Peter, and to the other disciple, whom Jesus loved, and saith unto them, They have taken away the Lord out of the sepulchre, and we know not where they have laid him."* Mary ran to them, because you have to understand, they didn't have *Twitter* in those days. They didn't have *Facebook*, they didn't have email, they didn't have *Instagram*, they didn't have *iPhones*, so Mary had to run. It was the only way to break the big news.

She hopes the disciples will know what to do. Maybe *they'll* have some answers. Maybe *they* can find him. So, she tells them. All of a sudden, the disciples take off—Peter first. You just know Peter is going to be first. But John is right behind him. In fact, John overtakes Peter. John gets to the tomb first and looks in. Verse 8 says something very interesting. *"Then went in also that other disciple, which came first to the sepulchre, and he saw, and believed."*

John looks into the tomb. Then Peter goes into the tomb and looks around. The unbelievable thing to me is that verse 10 says, *"Then the disciples went away again unto their own home."* Jesus is gone, and they're going home. You would think they would have stayed around, talked about it, tried to figure out, "Where do you think Jesus' body likely is?" But they went back home.

That's what happens when folks are undone and their world is turned upside down. They go back to their own homes, shut the doors and hide and hope that somehow or another this bad stuff will be over someday. But Mary kept hanging around. Mary did not leave the scene. *Love has a way of lingering.* Mary, snot running down her nose, eyes red and swollen, no body. Jesus is dead. But Mary lingers.

Love will do that.

CHAPTER TWENTY-SEVEN

"Friends love to linger"

I'VE FOUND SOMETIMES at church, when we have some wonderful services or Bible studies, the saints will just linger around. Sometimes I have to tell them, "Okay. We've got to go now." Then I get in my car, and First Lady and I find out they're lingering in the parking lot. Sometimes we'll tell them, if there are only a few females, "Get in your car and leave," because we can't leave women in the parking lot by themselves. But saints love to linger.

Friends love to linger.

Get a couple of friends around a good cup of coffee and some Danish rolls or some biscuits and jelly, and we will linger. Couples love to linger. They go to one of those romantic sites or go to a romantic dinner, and they love to linger. I haven't been able to treat my lovely wife to her birthday dinner because of COVID-19, but when I do it, it's going to be really nice, and we're going to linger.

Families love to linger. This is one of the difficulties now, because we're so used to being with each other at holidays. We're so used to sitting around the table, whether it's ham, whether it's turkey, whether it's fried chicken, whether it's baked fish, or whatever you may choose. We're used to lingering. Lingering means you have some important things to do and you will give it the time that's necessary to take care of it. In other words, you won't rush.

So, Mary is there after they leave. Verse 11 says, *"But Mary stood without at the sepulchre weeping: and as she wept, she stooped down, and looked into the sepulchre..."* What made Mary look? We don't know, but something happened, and Mary looked. *"...and seeth two angels in white sitting, the one at the head, and the other at the feet, where the body of Jesus had lain. And they say unto her, Woman, why weepest thou? She saith unto them, Because they have taken away my Lord, and I know not where they have laid him."* Understand that it says these angels are in white. Angels in the Bible were usually awesome creatures. Usually, they were dazzling. They looked fearsome. These angels were probably bright and large and powerful. Usually they'll say, "Fear not," because people who have not seen an angel are afraid. But here Mary does not even take note of who they were.

Now, I could imagine, if these were two brother angels, they would have said, "What y'all doing looking for someone who's alive and kicking in a tomb? Jesus is gone. He ain't here no more. Jesus is gone. He's nowhere to be found. So, don't come looking for a live hope in a dead situation." Verse 14: *"And when she had thus said, she turned herself back, and saw Jesus standing, and knew not that it was Jesus. Jesus saith unto her, Woman, why weepest thou? whom seekest thou? She, supposing him to be the gardener, saith unto him, Sir, if thou have borne him hence, tell me where thou hast laid him, and I will take him away."*

She still does not recognize Jesus. There's Jesus, there are angels, but Mary doesn't recognize any of them, because she's looking for her Lord. *"Jesus saith unto her,' Mary'."* And that's all it took. You know, they tell me that a child will always recognize two voices: the voice of Mama and the voice of Daddy. There was something about Jesus' voice when He called "Mary" that she recognized.

Mary was the one who had been delivered. Mary was wealthy and had helped in the ministry. It's believed that Mary was also older than Jesus, but Mary loved Jesus and Jesus loved

Mary. *"She turned herself, and saith unto him, Rabboni; which is to say, Master. Jesus saith unto her, Touch me not..."*

What you have to understand is that apparently, Mary touches the Lord. Apparently, Mary does grab ahold of Jesus, but Jesus says, *"[Don't touch me]; for I am not yet ascended to my Father..."* Mary was literally trying to grasp ahold of Jesus. Isn't that what faith is about? It is grasping ahold of those things which give us hope.

I looked up the word *grasping*, and it literally means to cling, to hold on, to firmly grip, to apprehend, to seize, to clutch, to clench, to clasp, to have a strong understanding, to have a strong urge, a pain to possess something, understanding that which is difficult, grasping something firmly, seizing, grasping.

Mary is saying, "I lost you once, and I don't want to lose you again. I have ahold of Jesus. At one time, I knew where He was at, 24/7, every day, and I don't want to lose Him. I watched Him being crucified. I watched Him die. But now He's alive, and I don't want to lose Him again."

Now, when I looked up *grasping*, the Holy Ghost said, "Also look up *grasping for straws*." That's a saying. The definition is to make a desperate attempt to salvage a bad situation, to depend on something that is useless, to make a futile attempt at something, a desperate attempt at saving oneself. If you look at what has been going on since COVID-19, we've been making all types of attempts.

What you hear today changes tomorrow. What you hear in the morning changes in the evening. What you hear in the evening changes at midnight. We're making a desperate attempt. We are trying to find everything we can, but we're grasping for straws. Man doesn't have a solution. They say we need ventilators, but now they're saying we have ventilators, but they aren't using the ventilators.

They set up ships, but now the ships are going back out to sea because we don't have enough folks for them. They have tests, but they're saying most folks have not received a test. We're trying to save the economy, but the money is not coming. Folks can't get the money because of a million questions. We are grasping for straws.

Mary's desire was just like us for the old relationship, for the old way, the old sounds, the old sights, the old touch. She's grasping, grasping, grasping for what is normal, but that isn't what Easter is about. Easter is about grasping His hope. Easter is about clinging to Him. It is about holding on to Him. It's about seizing Him. It's about embracing Him. It's about "I'll never let you go."

She's saying, "I lost you once, and I don't want to do it again." Her grief had been turned to joy. That's what the Bible says. "Weeping may endure for a night, but joy comes in the morning." Jesus lets her know, "Mary, things have changed. Your future will not be found in your past." In other words, Jesus said, "You can no longer cling to me physically, but now, Mary, you have to cling to me in a different way."

CHAPTER TWENTY-EIGHT

"Grasping Easter"

EACH YEAR, AS we observe Easter, we celebrate how Jesus turns our sorrows into joy and lets us know the worst is over. I wish I could tell the saints of God that you'll never feel pain, that you'll never have to deal with Covid-19 or that God's people will never die, but even this week, as I work on this book, a beloved African-American pastor passed away from COVID-19. I'd love to say that none of this will touch us and that we are completely immune to it.

I would love to say that you won't have to deal with unemployment. I would love to say you won't have to deal with losing your job. I would love to say that you won't have to deal with sorrow, disappointment, grief, sadness, and affliction. I would love to tell you that, but I would be lying. There's an age-old question: What do you do when hope dies? Can a dead hope be revived? Resurrection hope is about grasping. It's about clinging. It's about holding on to something.

God prompts me to ask: What were you holding on to before COVID-19? What's happening in the world is that we're finding out that we're holding on to a whole lot of stuff instead of the Lord. But now God has made this very simple, and now we have time to figure out what we were holding on to before COVID-19 and, more importantly, what we are holding on to now.

Let me tell you about hope. It is the same hope that healed the lepers. It is the same hope that gave sight to the blind. It is the same hope that calmed the raging sea. It is the same hope that told the wind "Peace, be still." It is the same hope that healed the lady with the issue of blood. It's the same hope that cast the demons out of Mary. It's the same hope that turned water into wine. Easter is grasping His hope. Not "hope so" but hope. A lot of folks hope that it will get better. "I hope so."

"Do you think we'll get rid of COVID-19?"

"I hope so."

"Do you think things will ever be the same?"

"I hope so."

This is not a "hope so" hope, because it's *His* hope. It is grasping *His* hope. I want to tell you something. Hope will do many wonderful things. It is the same hope that was brought to the courts and condemned Jesus on some trumped-up charges. It's the same hope that beat Him on Friday and bruised Him for our sins and our iniquities. It's the same hope that carried Him to the cross on Golgotha.

It's the same hope, as the old preachers say, that hung Him high and stretched Him wide. It's the same hope that nailed Him to the cross, the same hope that died on the cross, the same hope who looked at the thief and said, "Today, you'll be with me in paradise." It's the same hope who said, "Father, forgive them, for they know not what they do." It's the same hope that cried out "It is finished!" and the same hope that said, "I just need a borrowed tomb because I won't be there too long."

It's the same hope that went to hell, found the Devil, confronted Him, and said, "Now I'm going to be your plague. I'm going to be your COVID-19, -20, -21, -40, and -100. I'm going to be your Spanish flu. I'm going to be your cholera. I'm going to be your pandemic. I am your worst nightmare."

Jesus, the eternal God in human attire.

God in overalls stepped into hell. God with steel toes stepped into hell. God with a hard hat stepped into hell, but without a mask, without a shield, without a ventilator, and told death, "I am your plague. I am your pandemic. I am the breath." Satan had no ventilator. Satan started losing his breath, death started losing his breath, but they had no ventilator, because Jesus said, "I am the breath of life."

He called death to stop by hell and swallow up every disease. He swallowed up lupus. He swallowed up cancer. He swallowed up diabetes. He swallowed up high blood pressure. He swallowed up syphilis. He swallowed up COVID-19, and then told the Devil, "Give me the keys." He took the keys to death and hell and said, "I won't kill you, but I'm going to take away your sting." I hear the Word of God saying, "O death, where is your sting? And, grave, where is your victory? You can roar, but you don't have any teeth anymore, because God has snatched them out."

It is grasping *His* hope. We have a hope. That's what every Easter is about. Mary realized, "I have a hope now, but it's not 'hope so.' It's *His* hope. It's a lively hope. It's a living hope." Mary is now clutching. Mary is now seizing. Mary is now grasping. The Lord says that's what we have to do today. Verse 18: *"Mary Magdalene came and told the disciples that she had seen the Lord, and that he had spoken these things unto her. Then the same day at evening, being the first day of the week, when the doors were shut where the disciples were assembled for fear of the Jews, came Jesus and stood in the midst, and saith unto them, Peace be unto you."*

It is grasping His love, clinging to His love. It is grasping His peace that surpasses all understanding. Peace in the midst of a storm, in the midst of hell, in the midst of a world where it seems like nobody knows what to do. It's grasping His peace. "No, this isn't going to kill me. This won't destroy me. I will not have a nervous breakdown. I'm not going to lose it, because this joy that I have. The world didn't give it to me, and the world cannot take it away."

> "And when he had so said, he shewed unto them his hands and his side. Then were the disciples glad, when they saw the Lord. Then said Jesus to them again, Peace be unto you: as my Father hath sent me, even so send I you. And when he had said this, he breathed on them, and saith unto them, Receive ye the Holy Ghost..."

It is grasping His love. It is grasping His hope. It is grasping His peace. My brothers and sisters, this is the key to victory over COVID-19: *"Not by might, nor by power, but by my spirit, saith the Lord of hosts."* That's one of the reasons He told Mary, "You can't grab me, because now this is a spiritual thing. The paradigm has shifted. No longer is it physical; it's now spiritual. Mary, you have to be able to grasp and be able to comprehend."

It is the Spirit who changes pain to power and praise. It is the Spirit who changes suffering to strength and a song. It is the Spirit who takes misery and transforms it to might and miracles. It is the Spirit who takes depression and turns it into deliverance, determination, and dominance. It is the Spirit who takes worry and changes it into worship and wonder. It is the Spirit who takes anxiety and changes it into awe and amazement. It is the Spirit who takes doubt and turns it into a doxology. It is the Spirit who takes fear and changes it into faith and fortitude.

God is saying, "I have to ascend so the Holy Ghost can descend, and when it comes, you shall have power…power over depression, power over fear, power over COVID-19." God is saying, "I have to go, but grasp ahold of my Spirit. Press into me." What you will find out is that grief is nothing but a gateway to growth, and trouble is nothing but a trailway to triumph, and adversity is nothing but an avenue to the anointing, and pain is nothing but a pathway to prosperity, and suffering is nothing but a street to sanctification.

Grab ahold of Him. Grab ahold of His forgiveness. Grab ahold of His love. Grasp it. Cling to it. Seize it. Hold on to it, because God is saying, "Restoration is coming. Renewal is coming. You're going to be reenergized. A new life is coming."

Then God said, "Mary and the disciples, y'all have to grasp ahold of my agenda, because I have plans for y'all now. I have plans for y'all to turn the world upside down. Not just a hope for the future but a greater and a bigger assignment. Y'all are going to turn this world upside down. Don't hold on to me, Mary, because y'all have an assignment to go out and tell the world that He has risen. He is not in the grave anymore, but He has risen."

CHAPTER TWENTY-NINE

"Don't give up"

JESUS WAS GONE, and when He rose, He came up with the keys to death and hell. The God we serve is very much alive, so let the world know in the midst of COVID-19 that God is alive. God has risen. I'm grasping on the hope. I'm grasping on the peace. I'm grasping on the joy. I'm grasping on the love. God is letting me know He's not through with me, because God has a bigger and a better and a greater assignment for me.

Grasping Easter. Grasping faith. Grasping love. Clinging, holding, not letting go, clasping. In the midst of COVID-19, God is saying, "Cling to me. Hold on to me.

Grasp ahold of me, and there you'll find your peace. There you'll find your joy. There you'll find love." Some people say, "Well, Pastor Sykes, there's an elephant in the room, because Jesus let Thomas touch Him." He touched Jesus, because Thomas had to get ahold of faith. Mary couldn't touch Him because Mary had faith, but Jesus said, "It has to grow stronger." Mary believed. Thomas was doubting.

God always gives you what you need to get to where He wants you to be. God is saying the paradigm has shifted. It is no longer physical; it is spiritual. I want to say to every believer: in your life, the key to having your peace, the key to victory, the key to dealing with this mess-age... You have a message, and the message is if you grasp His hope, grasp His peace, grasp His faith, grasp His forgiveness, grasp His power, grasp His joy, in the end you will win, and you're going to be all right.

There was a movie many of us loved back in 1997 called *Titanic*. In that movie, there are two characters, Rose and Jack. As we all know, the *Titanic* hit an iceberg and started sinking. There's a scene where Rose and Jack are in the middle of the frozen Atlantic Ocean. They're holding dear to life, hoping somehow or another that they will survive. They are holding hands. Rose tries to tell Jack goodbye, because she believes that she's not going to make it; she's going to die. There are folks who are dealing with COVID-19, and they think, "I'm not going to make it. I'm going to die." Jack looks at Rose and says,

"Don't tell me goodbye. Don't you dare give up. Don't do it. You're going to get out of this. You're going to get out of it and have babies. You're going to get out of it and not only have babies, but you're going to watch them grow up."

He says, "You're not going to die in this frozen Atlantic water. You're going to die an old lady, warm in your own bed. But don't you die here. Promise me you won't give up no matter what happens, no matter how hopeless. Promise me that you'll never let go of the promise." He knew he was dying. He gave Rose what she needed to survive.

Both of them eventually start falling asleep. That's what happens when one suffers death from cold temperature. They go into a coma and start falling asleep. But Rose hears the voice from a rescue boat, and the voice is saying, "Can anybody hear me?" Rose looks around and realizes that Jack is asleep, that she's holding on to his hand. She tries to let go, but she can't. She's grasping Jack's hand. They're frozen together.

But she remembers what Jack told her. "Don't give up. You shall live. You shall have kids. You shall see them grow up. You shall go on and die warm in your own bed, but you won't die here." Rose for a moment felt like it was no use, and the voice was getting faint. All of a sudden, Rose realized, "If I'm going to live, I've got to stop clinging to a dead hope, to a dead situation."

Rose started blowing on her hands, trying to warm her hands up to get rid of the ice so she can pull her hands apart. Eventually, Rose lets go of Jack. She stops clinging to the dead hope. She stops clinging to the dead situation, and Rose starts crying out with a faint voice. A gentleman on the boat said, "I think I hear something." It was Rose saying, "I'm grasping life. I'm grasping hope. I'm grasping faith." Rose survived.

Today, God is saying, in the midst of COVID-19, "Don't give up. You shall have kids. You shall see your kids grow up. You will see them walk across the stage. You will see them become successful, God-fearing men and women."

God is saying to some of you in your 40s, 50s, 60s, and on, "You shall grow old, and you shall die warm in your own bed." God is saying, "You will graduate." There will be fellowship again in churches. We won't always have to wear a mask or gloves. David said, *I was glad when they said unto me, Let us go into the house of the Lord.* Someday, we're going to go into the house of the Lord and lift up our hands and run and sing.

You will be able to shop until you drop again.

You'll be able to get your hair done, get your nails done, get your toes done.

LeBron will be back on the courts.

You'll be able to root against the Cowboys and the Raiders again.

There will be March Madness again.

We'll smile. We'll have dinners together. We'll sit around the table. There will be plenty of toilet paper in the aisles. You'll get all that you want. You'll get all of the towels and Lysol wipes that you want. Someday we'll be able to hug, kiss, shake hands, love, and be together again.

Grasp ahold of hope!

Beloved, draw nigh
Rumbled in my valley
Pain seeped in parts of me
The ache grown roots
Anchored tethering me to lack
My tears have no receiver
I wailed bellowed obscenities
                    ...'You left me'

Beloved, take flight
Not with clipped wings
And fear born pathogens
dangling participles and modifiers
Caged be where I belong
                    ... 'but you
promised me I could dance free'

Then sing for me, Beloved
Like prayers of yesteryear
Where hope meandered with faith
Do you remember

No

You are the light, Beloved
Shown in the thickness of night
Thy kingdom stands before
Not veiled in secrecy
Dare see the offering

Darkness merely wrapped the gift,
Beloved

now See
        draw Nigh
                take Flight
                        then Sing
                                be the Light

"BELOVED," BY ERICA SUTHERLIN

· Made in the USA
Monee, IL
30 January 2021

59181667R00118